ANIMALS

Written by Angela Royston

•

HOW TO USE THIS BOOK

Each section of this book has stickers in its middle pages. Complete every page by finding the sticker that fits in each outline. Then read all about the different animals.

Funfax™ is an imprint of DK Publishing Inc., 375 Hudson Street, New York, NY 10014
Copyright © 1999 Funfax Ltd, an imprint of Dorling Kindersley Limited,
80 Strand, London WC2R 0RL
All rights reserved.

Deadly Dinosaurs and Mighty Dinosaurs first published as individual titles in 1999 by Funfax Ltd.
This edition published in 2003
Printed in China

Wild cats

Wild cats look beautiful, but these stealthy hunters have sharp claws and teeth.

Tiger
A tiger hunts for small animals at night. Its broken black stripes help it prowl unseen.

Tiger cub
This tiger cub has a big head and short legs. It is already learning how to hunt.

Puma
Pumas live in rain forests and mountains in North and South America.

White tiger
A few Indian tigers have white fur instead of orange-brown.

Largest cat
A male tiger is the largest and heaviest cat of all. Only a few tigers still live in the wild.

Cheetah
You can tell a cheetah by its spotted fur and long tail.

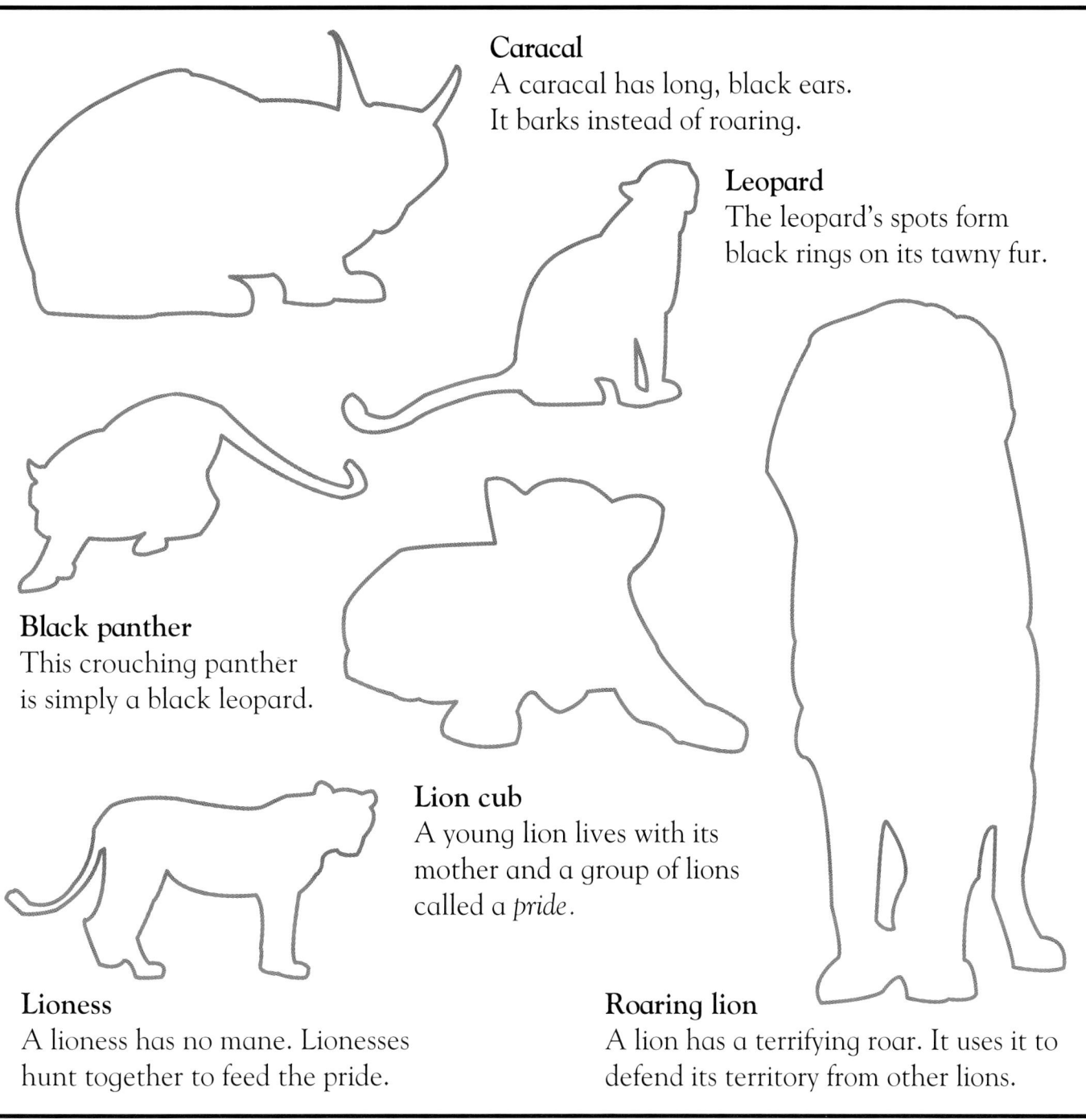

Caracal
A caracal has long, black ears.
It barks instead of roaring.

Leopard
The leopard's spots form
black rings on its tawny fur.

Black panther
This crouching panther
is simply a black leopard.

Lion cub
A young lion lives with its
mother and a group of lions
called a *pride*.

Lioness
A lioness has no mane. Lionesses
hunt together to feed the pride.

Roaring lion
A lion has a terrifying roar. It uses it to
defend its territory from other lions.

African animals

In Africa, huge grassy plains cover vast areas of land. Herds of large animals graze there.

Giraffe
The giraffe is the tallest land animal of all.

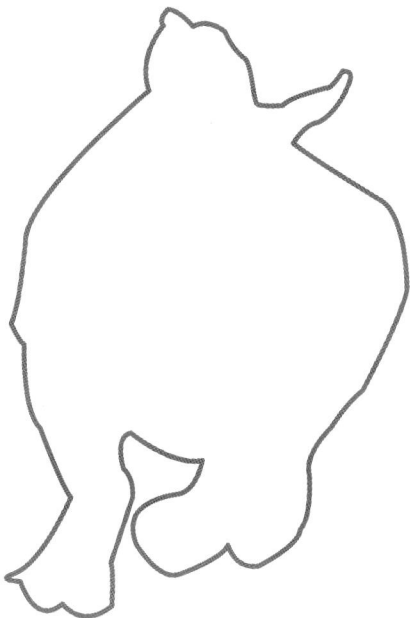

Zebra and foal
Every zebra has a different pattern of stripes, like an individual fingerprint.

Rhino
When a rhino is angry, it charges. Its large horn makes a lethal weapon.

Elephant mother and calf
The little elephant calf will grow up to be as big and heavy as its mother.

Rhino calf
This little rhino has not yet grown horns on its head.

There are extra stickers on these pages just for fun.

There are extra stickers on these pages just for fun.

Apes and monkeys

Most apes and monkeys live in tropical forests. They eat fruit and leaves and grip the branches with feet and hands.

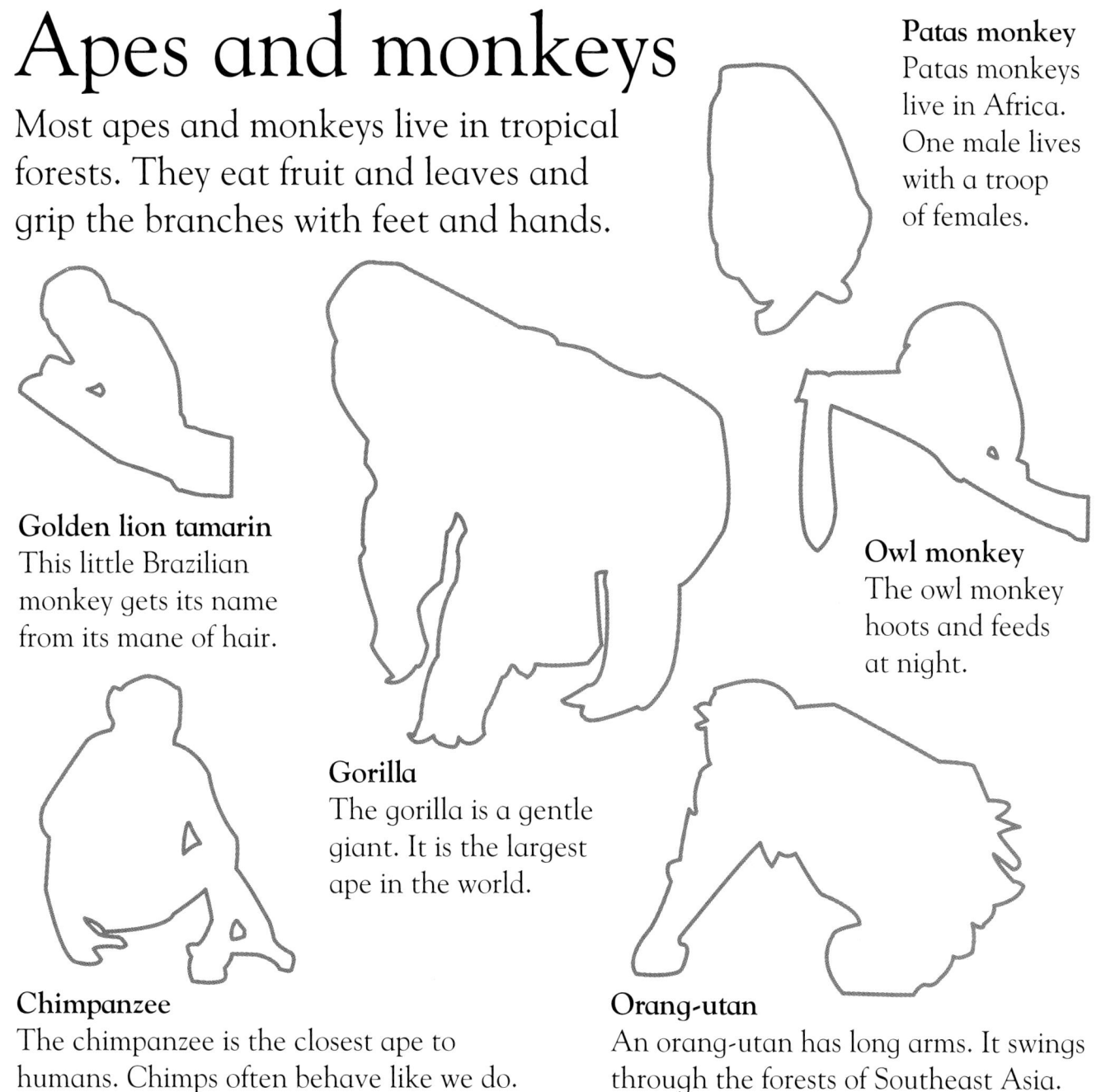

Patas monkey
Patas monkeys live in Africa. One male lives with a troop of females.

Golden lion tamarin
This little Brazilian monkey gets its name from its mane of hair.

Owl monkey
The owl monkey hoots and feeds at night.

Gorilla
The gorilla is a gentle giant. It is the largest ape in the world.

Chimpanzee
The chimpanzee is the closest ape to humans. Chimps often behave like we do.

Orang-utan
An orang-utan has long arms. It swings through the forests of Southeast Asia.

Water animals

Some mammals and large reptiles live in tropical lakes and rivers. Other mammals live in the sea.

Manatee
Manatees live in the sea. The female manatee feeds her young on her own milk.

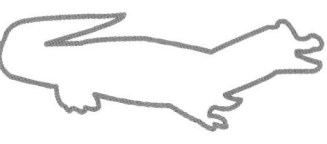

Caiman
A caiman is a crocodile from South America.

Alligator
An alligator has sharp teeth for catching prey.

Dugong
A dugong feeds on sea grass that grows in warm, shallow ocean waters.

Crocodile
A crocodile has a strong tail which it lashes to swim fast through the water.

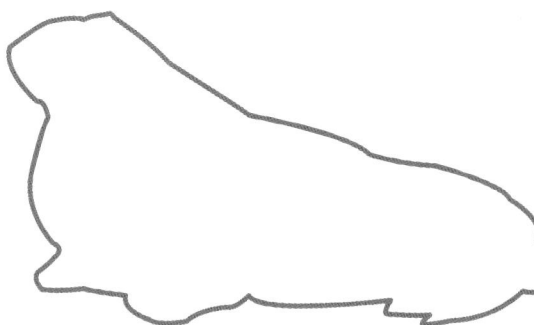

Hippopotamus
This African mammal loves to wallow in muddy water.

Walrus
This huge mammal has layers of fat called blubber. It is an excellent swimmer.

Cool creatures

Some animals live in the freezing water and on land around the North and South Poles.

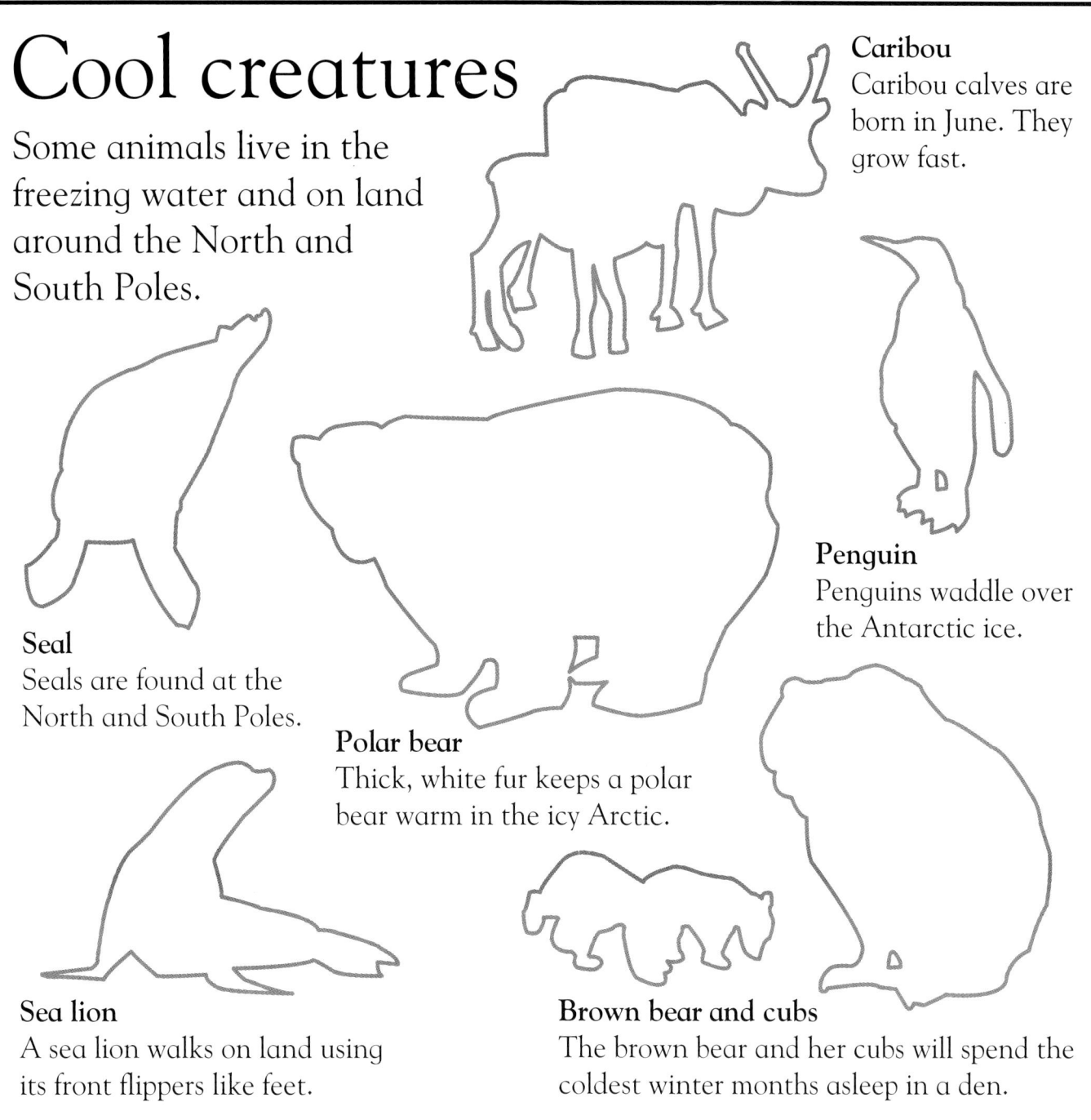

Caribou
Caribou calves are born in June. They grow fast.

Penguin
Penguins waddle over the Antarctic ice.

Seal
Seals are found at the North and South Poles.

Polar bear
Thick, white fur keeps a polar bear warm in the icy Arctic.

Sea lion
A sea lion walks on land using its front flippers like feet.

Brown bear and cubs
The brown bear and her cubs will spend the coldest winter months asleep in a den.

Australian animals

Some unusual animals, called *marsupials*, live in Australia. They carry their babies in a special pouch.

Wombat
Wombats use their powerful front legs to dig long burrows under the ground.

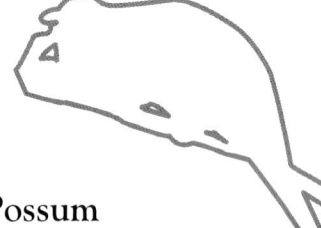

Possum
This little possum lives in the trees. It is related to the American opossum.

Wallaby and joey
The joey likes to hop into its mother's pouch.

Dingo
Dingos are wild dogs. They roam in packs and prey on sheep.

Koala
A koala clings to tree trunks. It only eats the leaves of eucalyptus trees.

Two kangaroos
Kangaroos use their long tails to balance.

SHARKS AND WHALES

The great white shark

The great white shark is the largest shark that hunts live food. It can eat a seal whole!

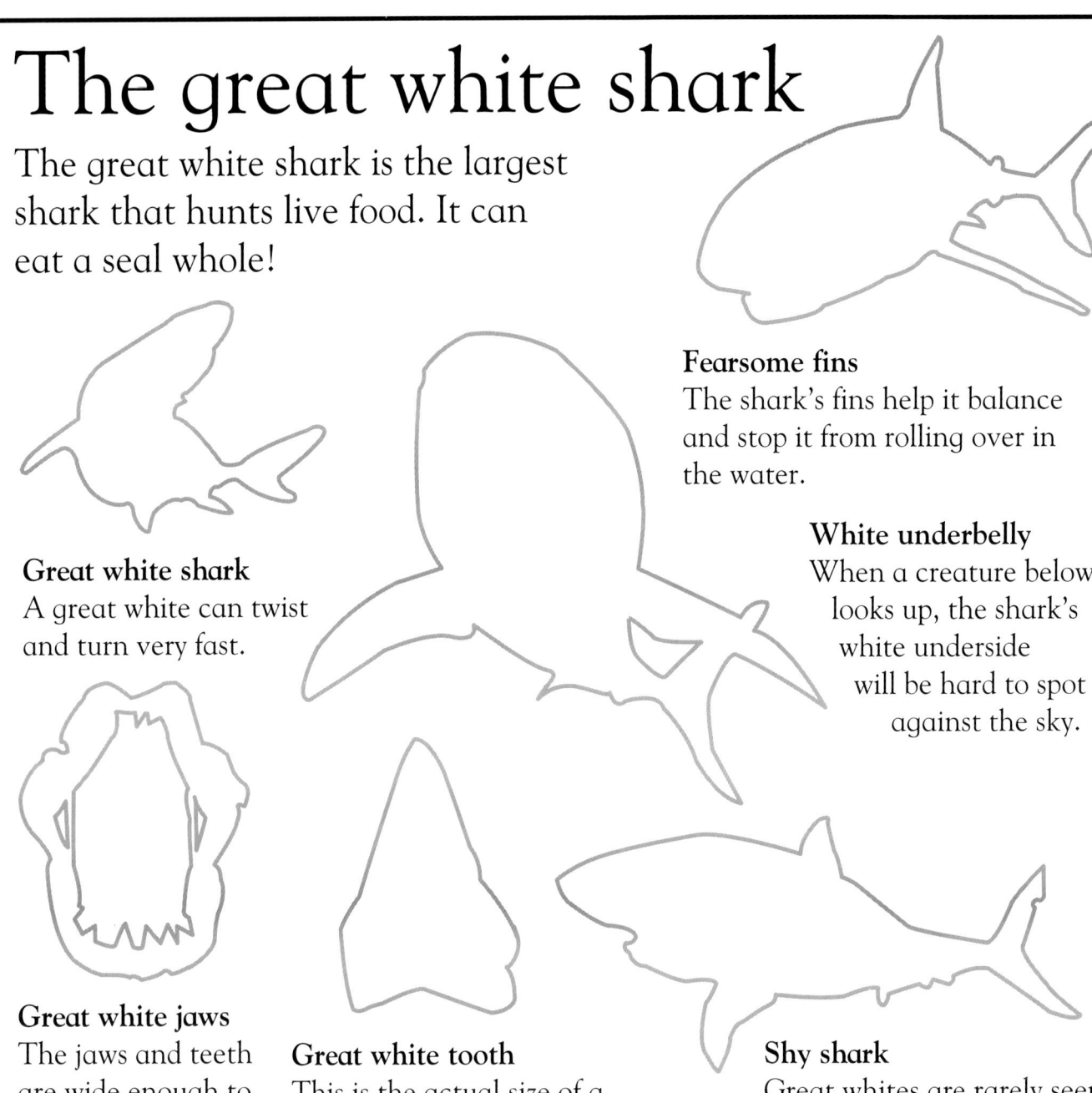

Great white shark
A great white can twist and turn very fast.

Fearsome fins
The shark's fins help it balance and stop it from rolling over in the water.

White underbelly
When a creature below looks up, the shark's white underside will be hard to spot against the sky.

Great white jaws
The jaws and teeth are wide enough to crawl through.

Great white tooth
This is the actual size of a great white shark's tooth.

Shy shark
Great whites are rarely seen and seldom attack people.

On the move

Some sharks speed through the water; others hide on the seabed. Their tail and fins help them move.

Swell shark
A swell shark lurks on the seabed. It swells up to wedge itself into a crack.

Spinner shark
This shark spins around like a spinning top to confuse its prey.

Black tip reef shark
A black tip reef shark flicks its tail to thrust it through the water. The fins help it steer.

Leopard shark
The leopard shark's large, black spots help it hide on the seabed.

Starry smooth-hound
The starry smooth-hound has wide side fins, like wings, which stop it from sinking.

Gentle giants

The whale shark is the world's largest fish. Some of its relatives, shown here, are much smaller.

White-spotted bamboo shark
This shark's white spots are hard to see on the seabed.

Brown-banded bamboo shark
Small sharks such as this one live on the seabed.

Epaulette shark
This shark has tiny teeth no bigger than match heads.

Whale shark
The largest whale shark is longer than a bus. It has rough skin and a huge tail.

Nurse shark's snout
Two spikes on the nurse shark's snout are used to probe for food in the sand.

Nurse shark
The nurse shark feeds on shrimps and other animals that live in the seabed.

Odd-shaped sharks

Sharks are not all sleek, streamlined creatures. Some of them have a strange-shaped head and body.

Wobbegong
A wobbegong has tassels on its head, like seaweed.

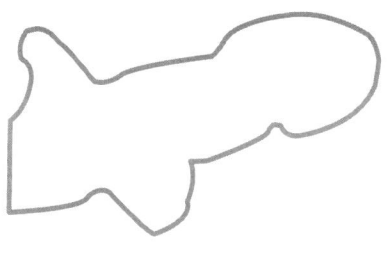

Bonnethead shark
A bonnethead shark has a wide, flat head. The shape may help to keep it afloat.

Angel shark
An angel shark is very flat with wide side fins.

Horn shark
Horn sharks are also called bullheads. They have horn-shaped spines on their back.

Thresher shark
The thresher shark uses its long tail to stun its prey.

The angel's tail
The angel shark flaps its tail from side to side to push itself along.

Giant whales

Whales are mammals like cows, dogs, seals, and humans. The blue whale is the largest mammal and the largest ever animal.

Sperm whale
A sperm whale has a huge head and dives deep to hunt for prey.

Humpback whale
A humpback whale has a knobbly head and long, black and white flippers.

Gray whale
A gray whale swims along the seabed looking for food.

Blue whale
Blue whales, like many big whales, have baleen plates instead of teeth. They gulp huge amounts of water and filter out tiny fish and sea creatures.

Baleen whale
Baleen plates are like brushes with fringes of bristles. They stretch to take in gulps of water.

More whales

There are about 78 species, or groups, of whale. Here are a few of the smaller ones.

Pilot whale
Pilot whales get their name from their habit of swimming in front of ships as they sail along.

Pygmy right whale
The pygmy right whale is the smallest baleen whale and is not often seen.

Narwhal
The narwhal's long tusk is an extra-long tooth. It is usually the males that have one; but occasionally a female does, too.

Pygmy sperm whale
The pygmy sperm whale is not much longer than your bed. It lives in the open ocean and dives deep for food.

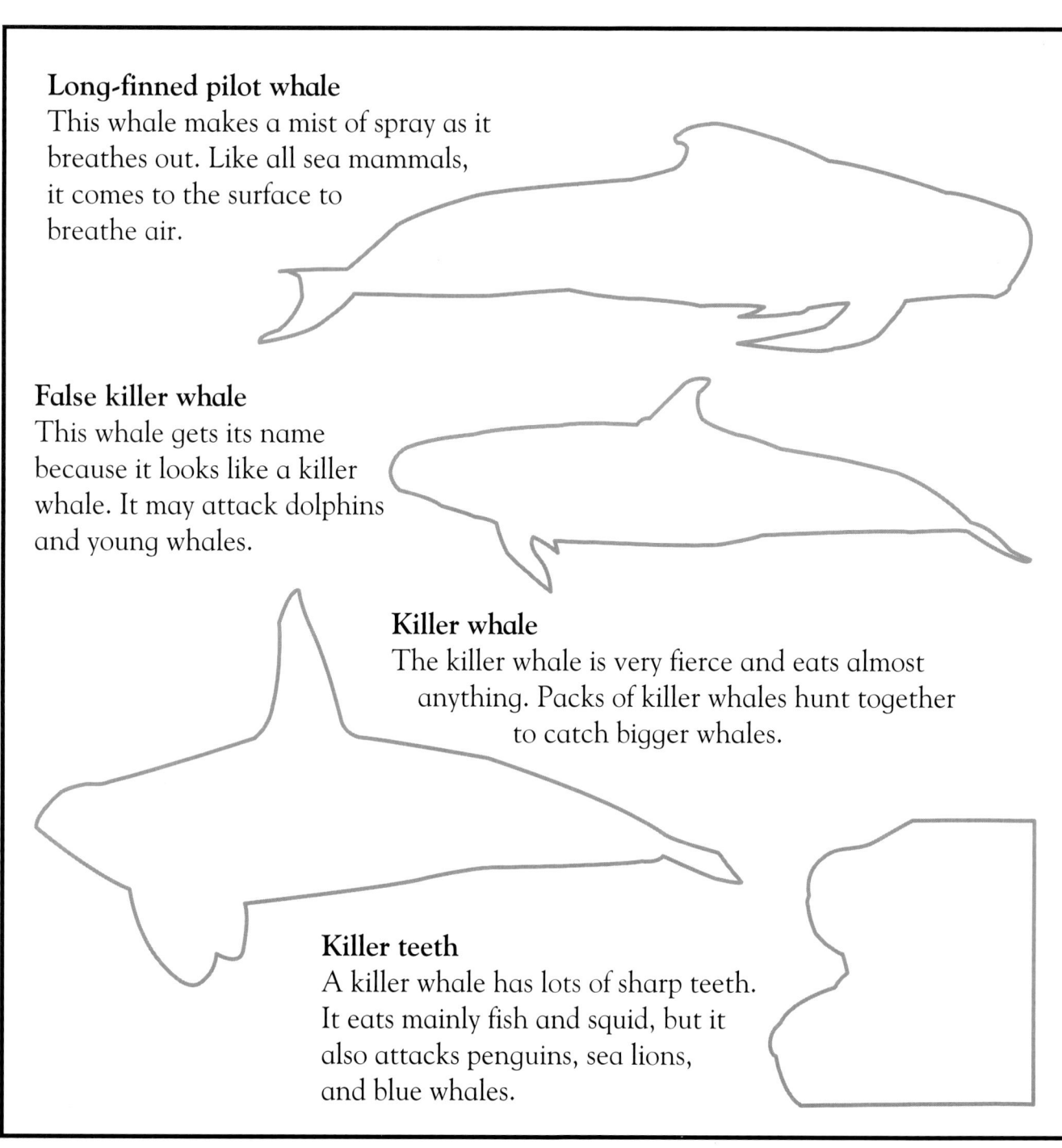

Long-finned pilot whale
This whale makes a mist of spray as it breathes out. Like all sea mammals, it comes to the surface to breathe air.

False killer whale
This whale gets its name because it looks like a killer whale. It may attack dolphins and young whales.

Killer whale
The killer whale is very fierce and eats almost anything. Packs of killer whales hunt together to catch bigger whales.

Killer teeth
A killer whale has lots of sharp teeth. It eats mainly fish and squid, but it also attacks penguins, sea lions, and blue whales.

CREEPY CRAWLIES

Beetles and bugs

Beetles have a pair of hard wings folded across their back. Bugs have a long tube for sucking up food.

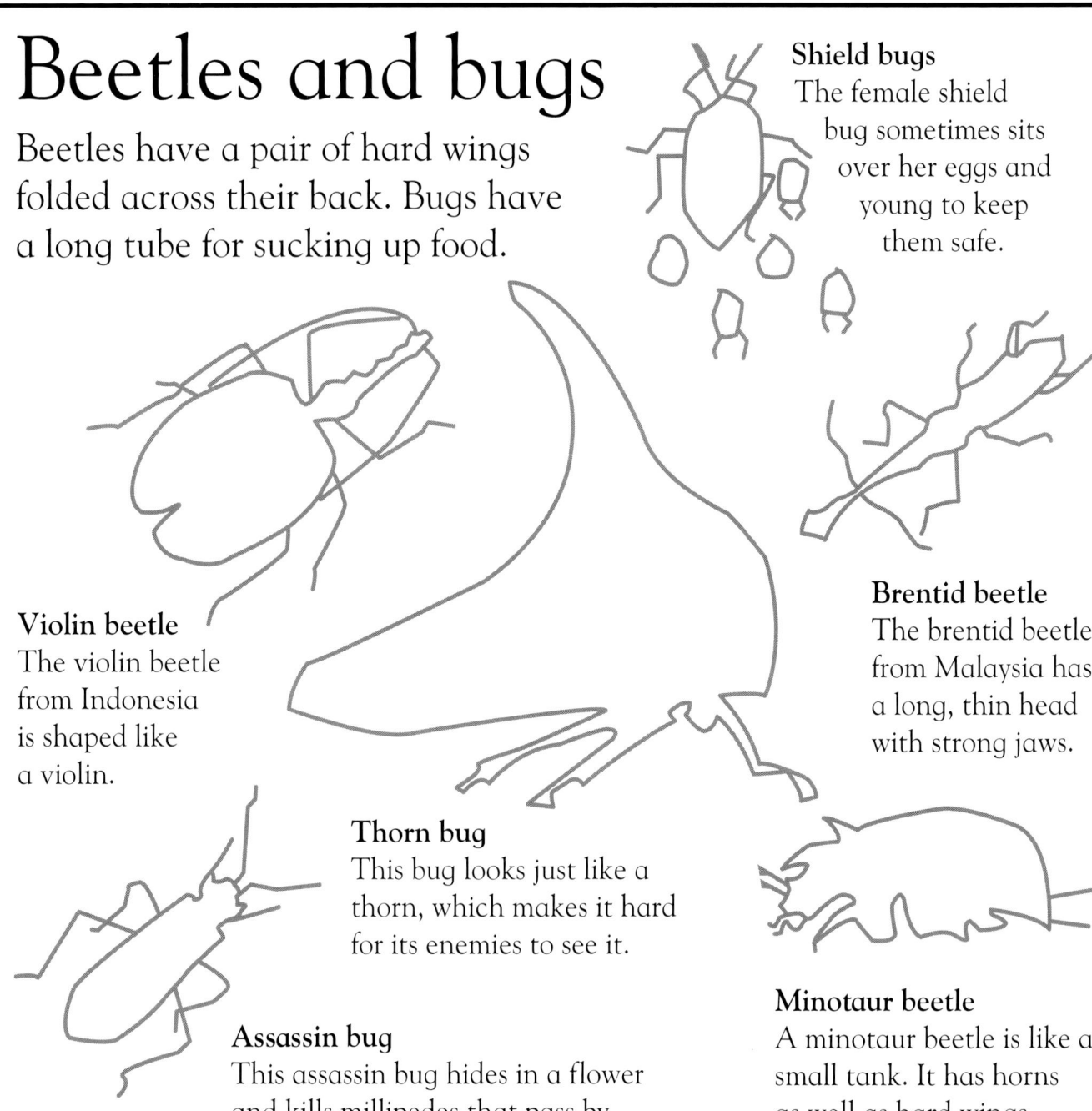

Shield bugs
The female shield bug sometimes sits over her eggs and young to keep them safe.

Brentid beetle
The brentid beetle from Malaysia has a long, thin head with strong jaws.

Violin beetle
The violin beetle from Indonesia is shaped like a violin.

Thorn bug
This bug looks just like a thorn, which makes it hard for its enemies to see it.

Minotaur beetle
A minotaur beetle is like a small tank. It has horns as well as hard wings.

Assassin bug
This assassin bug hides in a flower and kills millipedes that pass by.

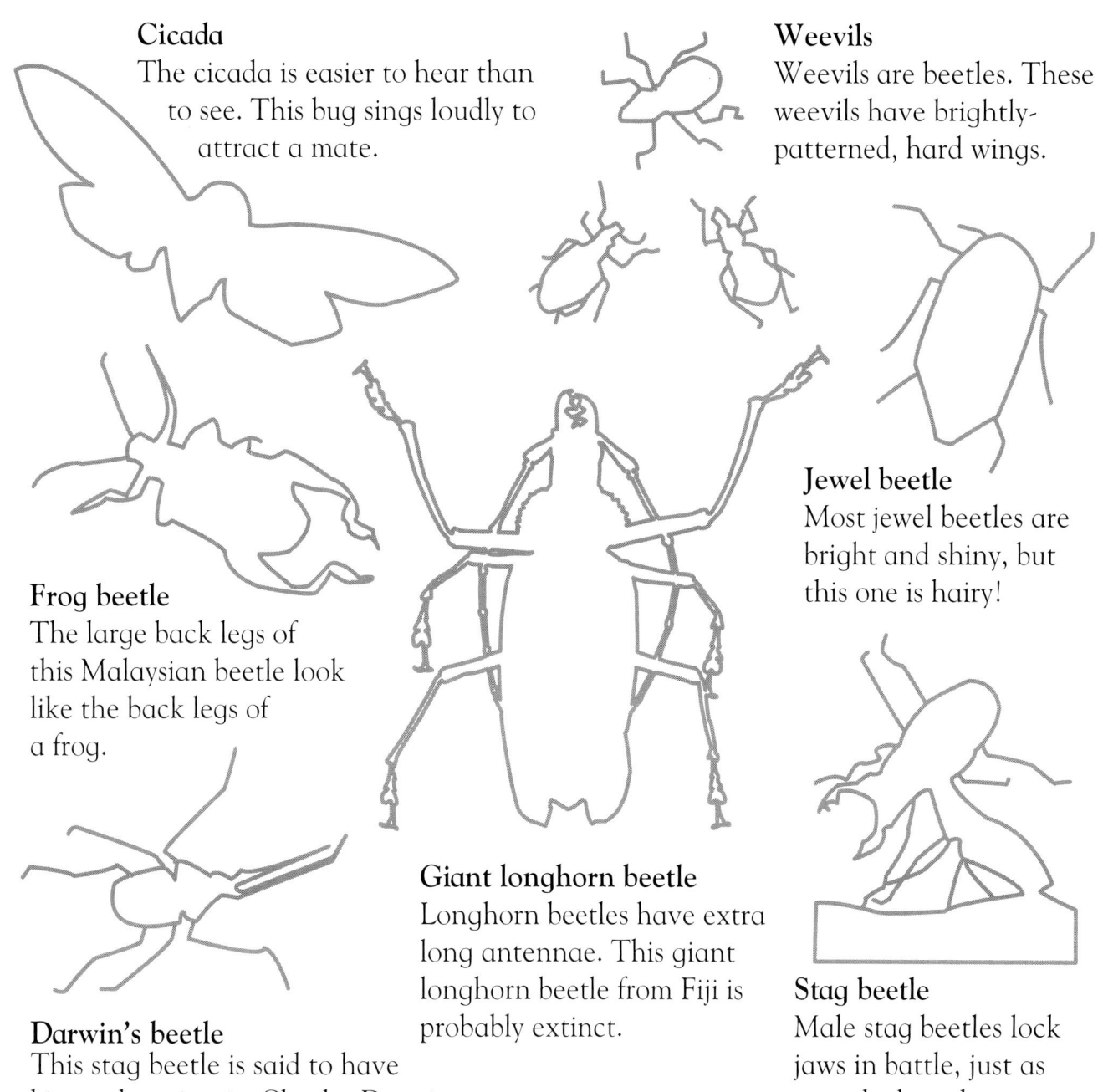

Cicada
The cicada is easier to hear than to see. This bug sings loudly to attract a mate.

Weevils
Weevils are beetles. These weevils have brightly-patterned, hard wings.

Jewel beetle
Most jewel beetles are bright and shiny, but this one is hairy!

Frog beetle
The large back legs of this Malaysian beetle look like the back legs of a frog.

Giant longhorn beetle
Longhorn beetles have extra long antennae. This giant longhorn beetle from Fiji is probably extinct.

Stag beetle
Male stag beetles lock jaws in battle, just as stags lock antlers.

Darwin's beetle
This stag beetle is said to have bitten the scientist Charles Darwin.

Wasps and bees

Wasps and bees are easy to recognize because of their narrow waist. Many bees and wasps can sting.

Jewel wasp
A jewel wasp is shiny and green with long antennae.

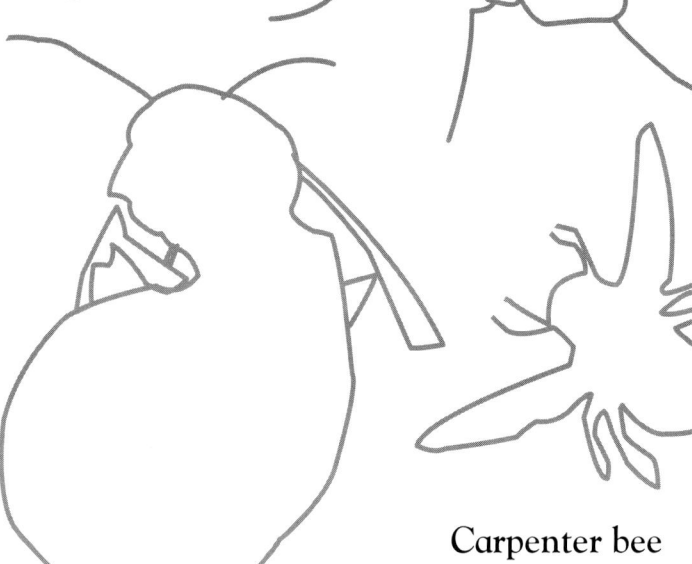

Queen wasp
The queen wasp makes a nest and lays her eggs. The eggs become worker wasps.

Hornet
Hornets are the largest wasps in Europe. They give a very painful sting.

Carpenter bee
The Asian carpenter bee is the largest bee in the world.

Tarantula hawk
This wasp is the largest in the world. It kills big spiders.

Hunting wasp
This bright green wasp hunts crickets in India and Borneo.

Flies and ants

Flies are insects with only one pair of wings. Ants are insects which live in groups called colonies.

Male driver ant
The male driver ant has wings and looks like a sausage!

Mydid fly
The mydid fly from South America is probably the largest fly in the world.

Queen driver ant
The queen driver ant is much bigger than the workers.

African fly
This fly has patterned wings.

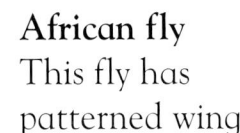

Long-legged crane fly
Crane flies have long legs. This Chinese one is among the largest.

Dung flies
These dung flies from Europe usually breed on wet cow dung.

Robber fly
A robber fly lies in wait and kills other insects as they fly past.

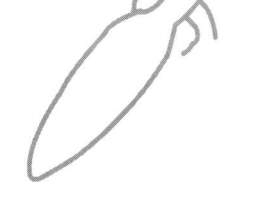

Waterbirds

Waterbirds include ducks and geese. Many have webbed feet for swimming in ponds, lakes, and rivers.

Male mandarin duck
The male mandarin has a bushy crest on top of his head.

Smew
A smew floats on the water and dives down to catch fish to eat.

Female mandarin
The female mandarin, like all female ducks, has duller plumage than the male.

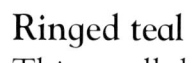

Ringed teal
This small duck dabbles for food at the surface of the water.

Swan
The swan is the largest, heaviest bird on lakes, ponds, and rivers.

Mallard
Mallard ducks often live and breed in city parks.

Red-breasted goose
Geese are bigger than ducks. This rare goose lives in Russia and Siberia.

Waders

Wading birds live and feed around the edge of water. Most of them have long legs and a long bill.

Pied avocet
This elegant bird lives on shores and around the edge of salty lagoons.

Scarlet ibis
The scarlet ibis lives in flocks on the coast of South America.

Flamingo
A flamingo has a long neck and long legs. It dips its bill into the mud to sift for food at the bottom of shallow lakes where it lives.

Black crake
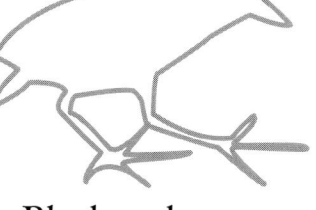
This small bird has wide feet to stop it from sinking into the mud.

Black-necked stilt

This American bird lives on coasts and in marshes.

Wattled jacana
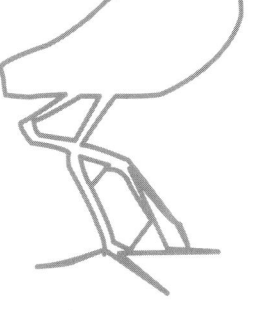
A jacana, also called a lily trotter, can run across lily pads on its long, thin toes.

Tropical birds

Birds with bright feathers live in the tall rainforest trees. They peck at fruit with their sharp bills.

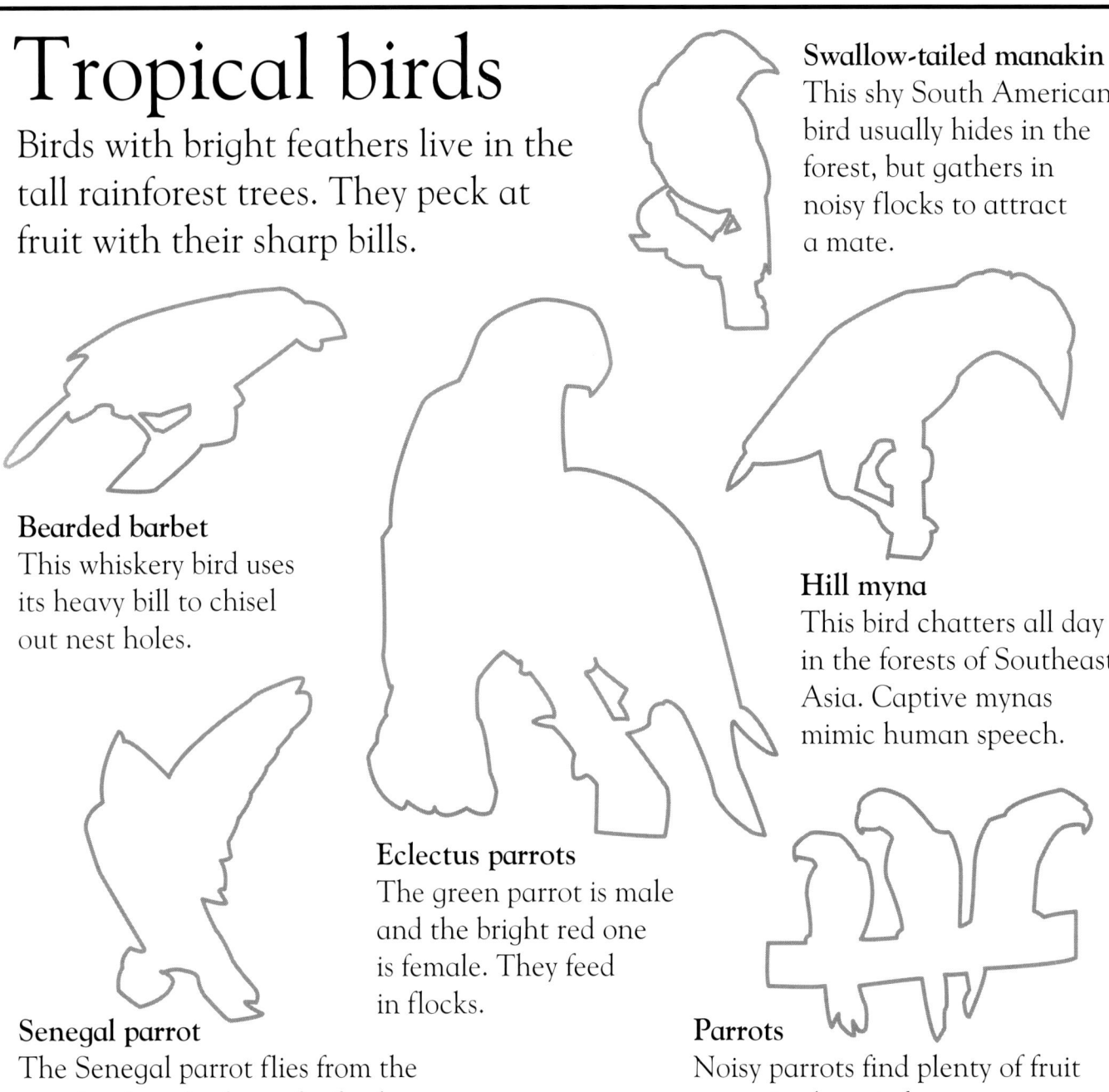

Swallow-tailed manakin
This shy South American bird usually hides in the forest, but gathers in noisy flocks to attract a mate.

Bearded barbet
This whiskery bird uses its heavy bill to chisel out nest holes.

Hill myna
This bird chatters all day in the forests of Southeast Asia. Captive mynas mimic human speech.

Eclectus parrots
The green parrot is male and the bright red one is female. They feed in flocks.

Senegal parrot
The Senegal parrot flies from the grassland to the forest for food.

Parrots
Noisy parrots find plenty of fruit to eat in the rainforests.

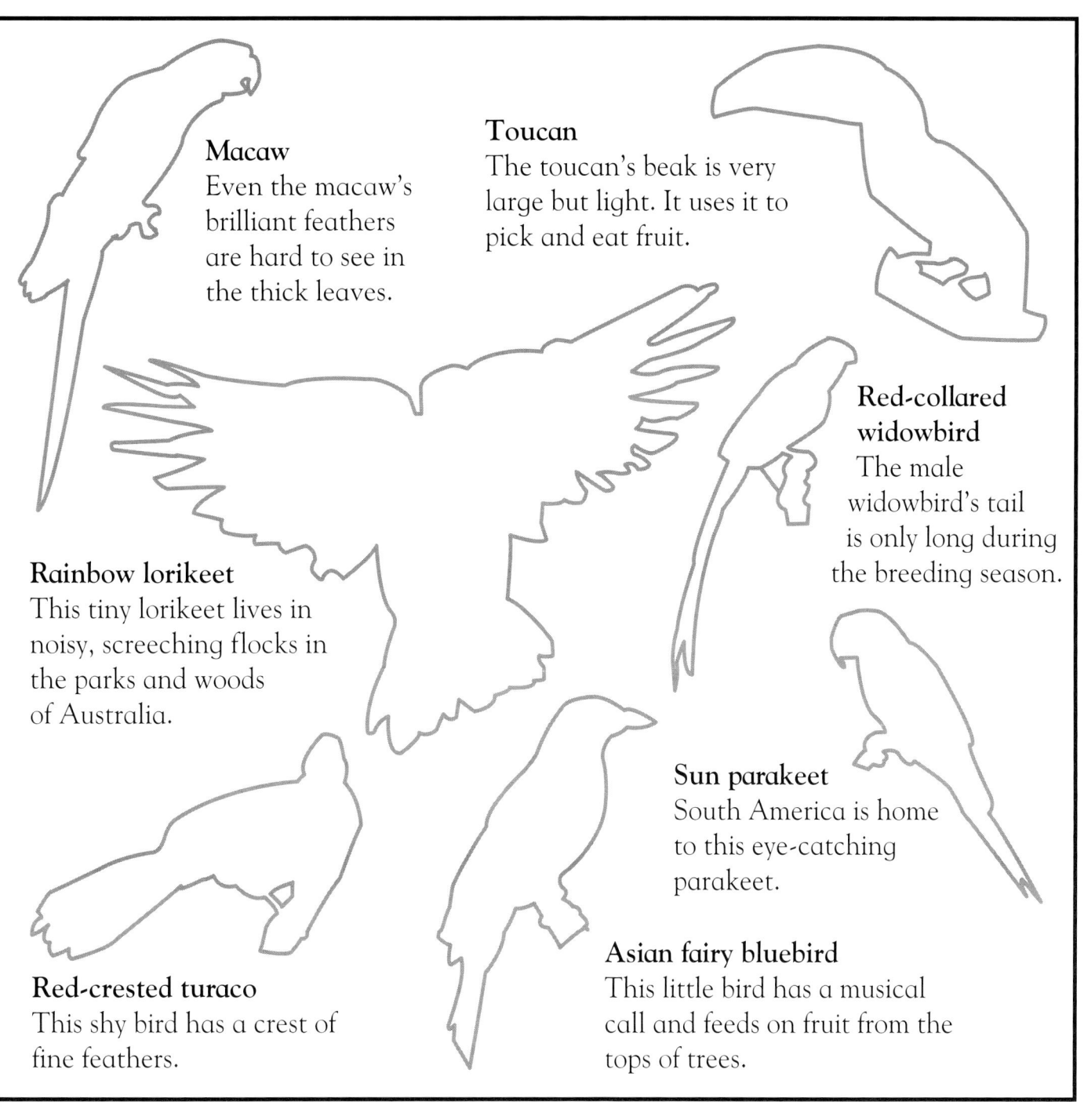

Macaw
Even the macaw's brilliant feathers are hard to see in the thick leaves.

Toucan
The toucan's beak is very large but light. It uses it to pick and eat fruit.

Red-collared widowbird
The male widowbird's tail is only long during the breeding season.

Rainbow lorikeet
This tiny lorikeet lives in noisy, screeching flocks in the parks and woods of Australia.

Sun parakeet
South America is home to this eye-catching parakeet.

Red-crested turaco
This shy bird has a crest of fine feathers.

Asian fairy bluebird
This little bird has a musical call and feeds on fruit from the tops of trees.

Birds of prey

Birds of prey are hunters. They grab small animals with their sharp talons and carry them off to eat.

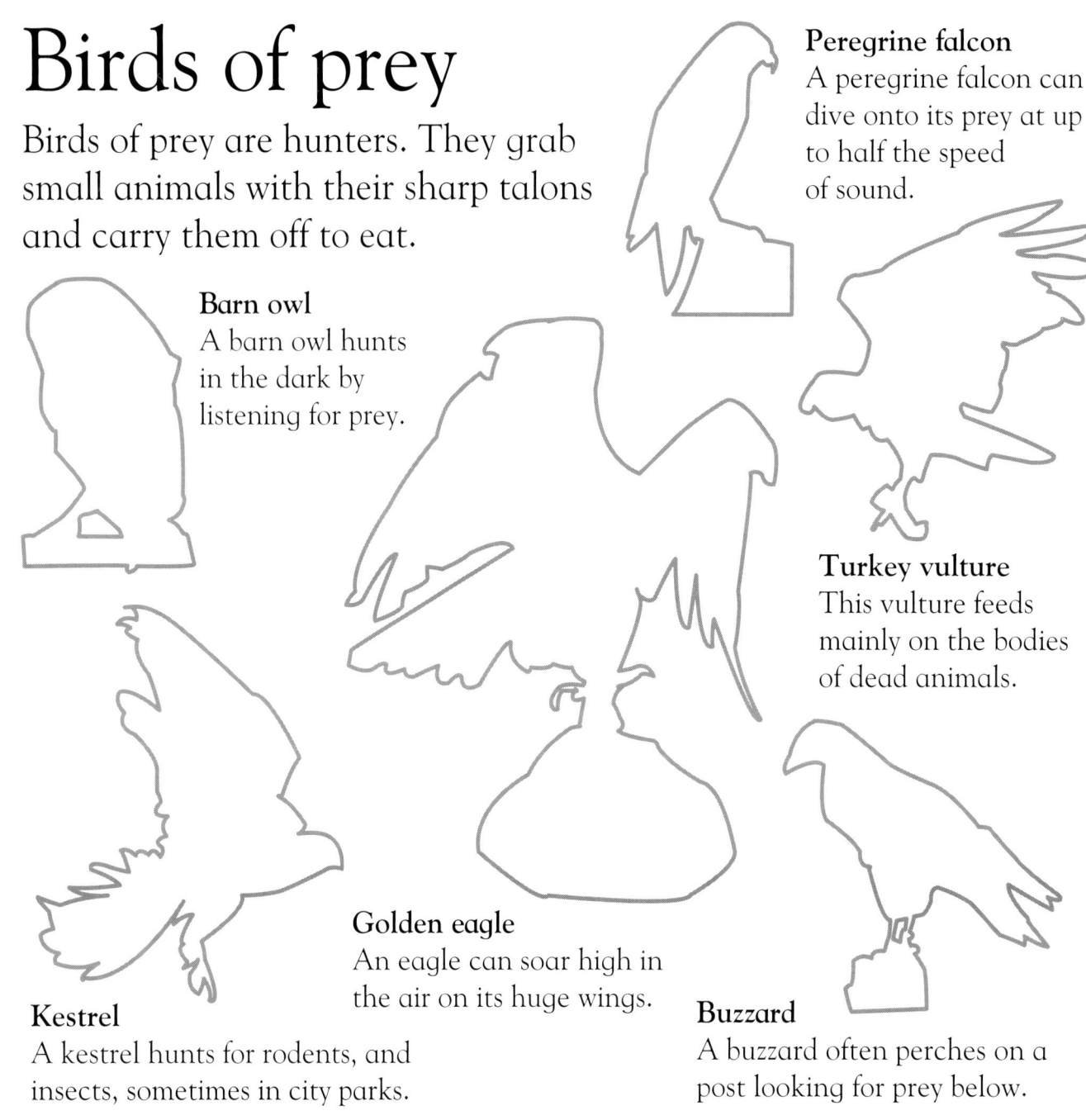

Peregrine falcon
A peregrine falcon can dive onto its prey at up to half the speed of sound.

Barn owl
A barn owl hunts in the dark by listening for prey.

Turkey vulture
This vulture feeds mainly on the bodies of dead animals.

Golden eagle
An eagle can soar high in the air on its huge wings.

Kestrel
A kestrel hunts for rodents, and insects, sometimes in city parks.

Buzzard
A buzzard often perches on a post looking for prey below.

Little birds

Most of these little birds are often seen in parks and gardens. They perch on twigs and sing loudly.

Nightingale
The nightingale is dull brown. It can sing many different songs.

Bullfinch
A bullfinch feeds on fruit and flower buds.

Hummingbird
The tiny hummingbird hovers in front of flowers as it feeds on their nectar.

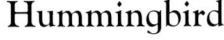

House sparrow
A house sparrow eats seeds, worms, fruit, and kitchen scraps.

Common starling
Starlings live in cities and roost in large, noisy flocks.

Blue tit
A blue tit is often seen in European parks and gardens.

Robin
The Eurasian robin puffs out its bright red breast when it is angry.

Seabirds

Some seabirds live in the coldest places. Others fly over oceans or live along coasts and farther inland.

Pelican
Pelicans catch fish in their long bill and swallow them whole.

Inca tern
This bird dives to snatch fish from the surface of the sea.

Emperor penguins
Emperor penguins live in the seas around Antarctica. They move onto the ice in winter to breed.

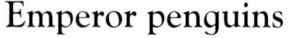

Herring gull
A herring gull lives both near the coast and inland.

Cormorant
A cormorant often spreads its wings to dry its wet feathers.

Oystercatcher
An oystercatcher lays its eggs in a hollow on the beach.

Ringed plover
This small bird is hard to spot among pebbles.

HORSES AND PONIES

Coat colours

A horse's colour is decided by the colour of its coat, its mane, its tail and its skin. Here are a few of the hundreds of possibilities.

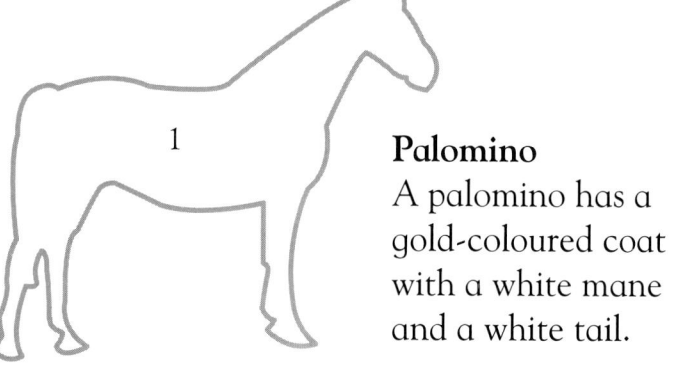

Palomino
A palomino has a gold-coloured coat with a white mane and a white tail.

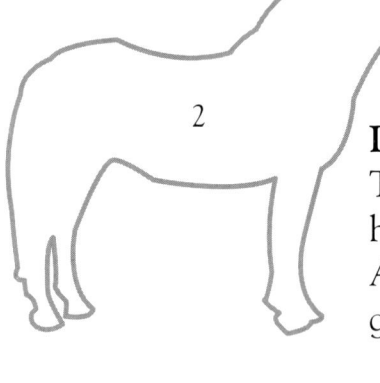

Dun
This dun has yellow hair and black skin. A blue dun's hair is grey or black.

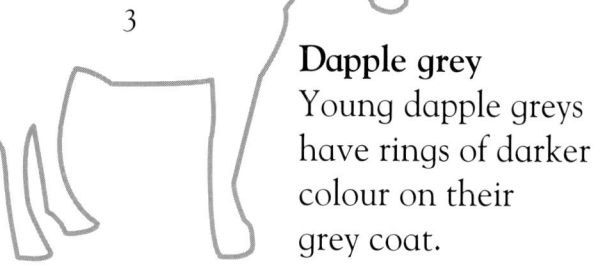

Dapple grey
Young dapple greys have rings of darker colour on their grey coat.

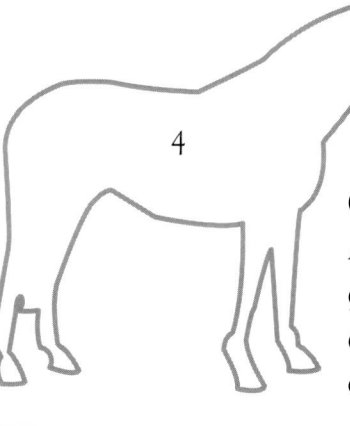

Chestnut
A chestnut has golden hair, mane and tail. The shade of gold varies.

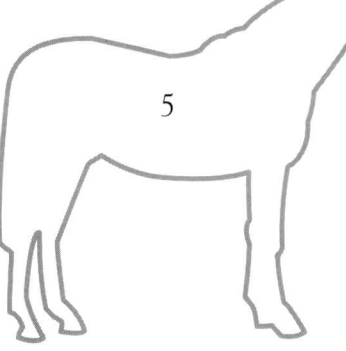

Bay
A bay has a reddish-brown to dark gold coat, with a black mane, tail and legs.

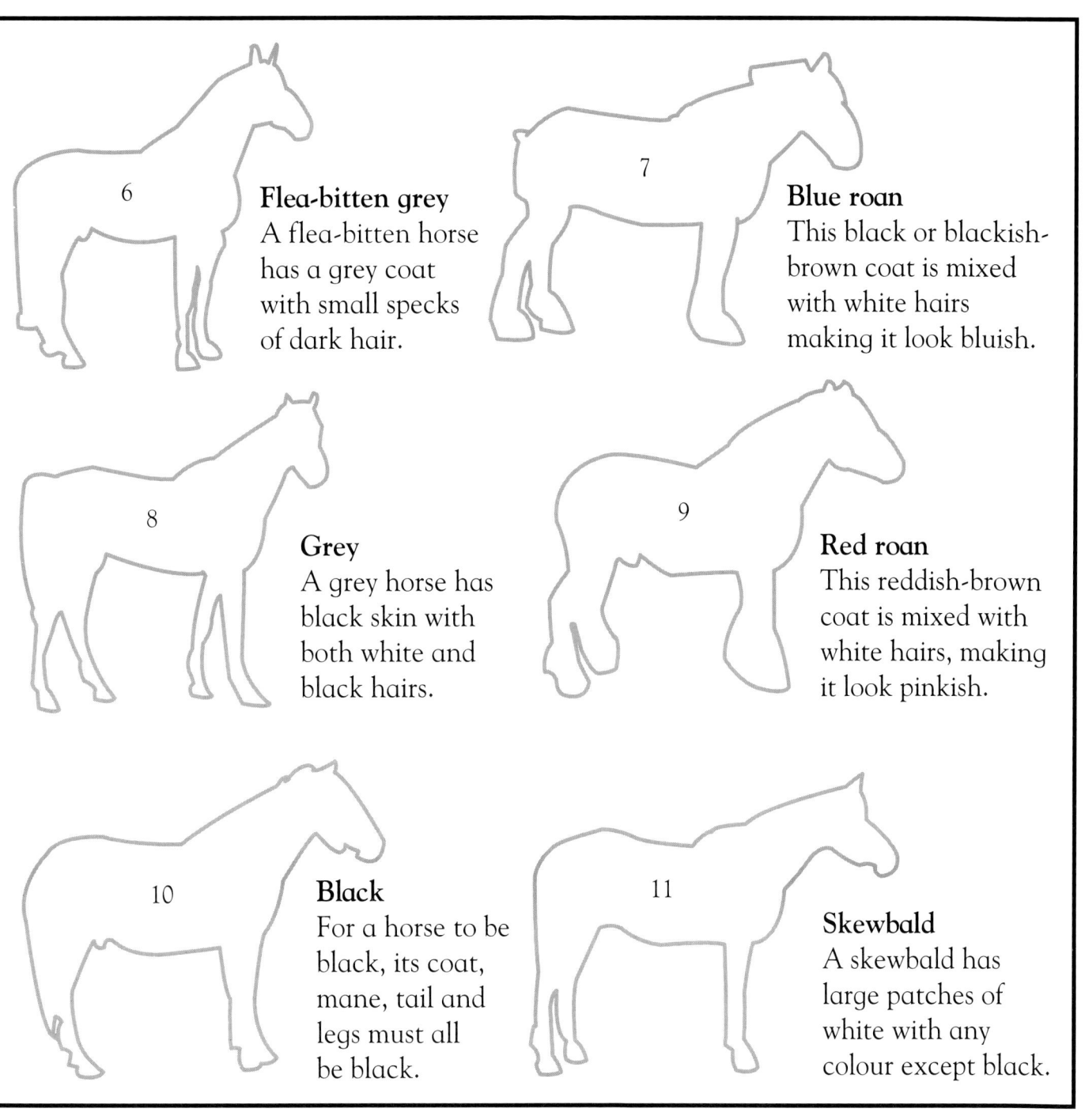

Flea-bitten grey
A flea-bitten horse has a grey coat with small specks of dark hair.

Blue roan
This black or blackish-brown coat is mixed with white hairs making it look bluish.

Grey
A grey horse has black skin with both white and black hairs.

Red roan
This reddish-brown coat is mixed with white hairs, making it look pinkish.

Black
For a horse to be black, its coat, mane, tail and legs must all be black.

Skewbald
A skewbald has large patches of white with any colour except black.

Your pony

Would you like to own a pony? It takes a lot of money and hard work! You have to enjoy looking after it.

Washing a pony
You only need to wash a pony if you are getting it ready to go to a show.

Grooming your pony
Grooming a pony every day with special brushes keeps its coat clean and healthy.

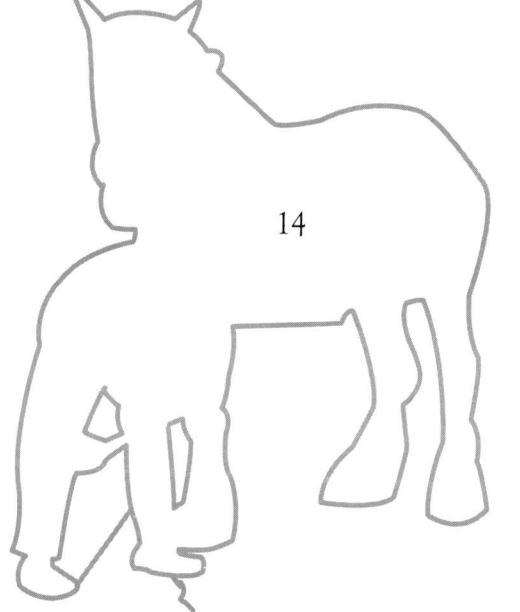

Trotting
Trotting is difficult. Riding lessons teach you how to ride and control the pony.

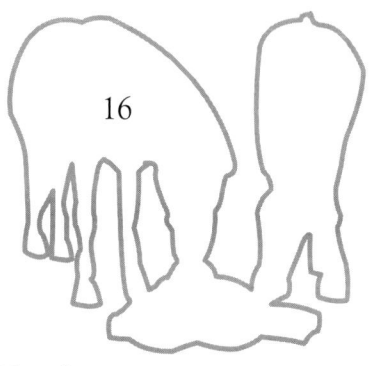

New shoes
A farrier checks the horse's hooves and fits new metal shoes.

Feeding
Ponies and horses feed mainly on grass or hay (which is dried grass).

Galloping
Galloping is fun, but you need to be a good rider first.

24

23

37

29

31

21

36

30

22

32

6

11

10

20

12

16

13

9

5

2

8

3

17

1

4

1

14

19

7

Working horses

For hundreds of years horses carried people and pulled carriages and carts. Today only a few horses still work.

Harness racing
This horse pulls a light cart and a driver in a fast race.

18

Drum horse
A drum horse has to be calm in parades.

19

20

21

Polo
Polo ponies are fast and brave. They can twist and turn.

22

Horse and cart
Two horses work together to pull this loaded cart.

Rodeo
At a rodeo, cowboys on horseback lasso young cattle and demonstrate other skills.

Breeds

There are more than 160 breeds. Light horses are good for riding and racing. Strong, heavy horses pull loads.

Andalucian
An Andalucian is agile and gentle. It is good for jumping and dressage.

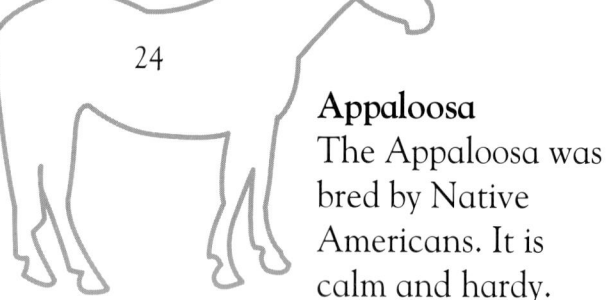

Appaloosa
The Appaloosa was bred by Native Americans. It is calm and hardy.

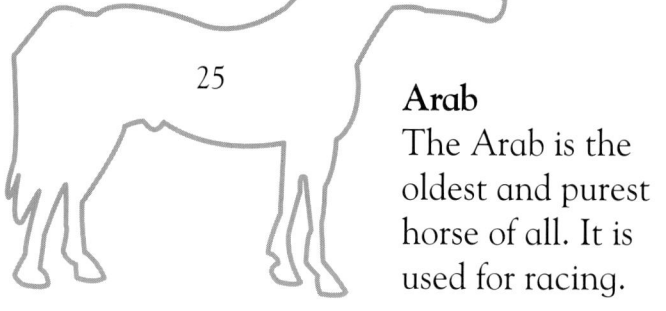

Arab
The Arab is the oldest and purest horse of all. It is used for racing.

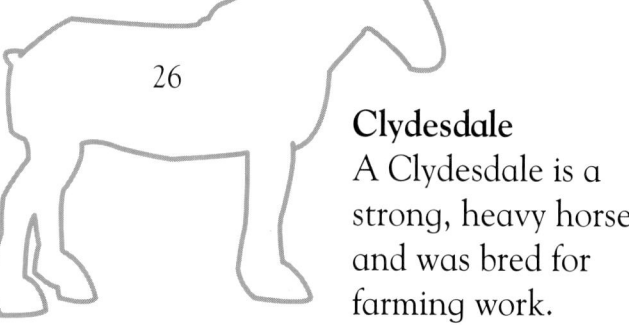

Clydesdale
A Clydesdale is a strong, heavy horse and was bred for farming work.

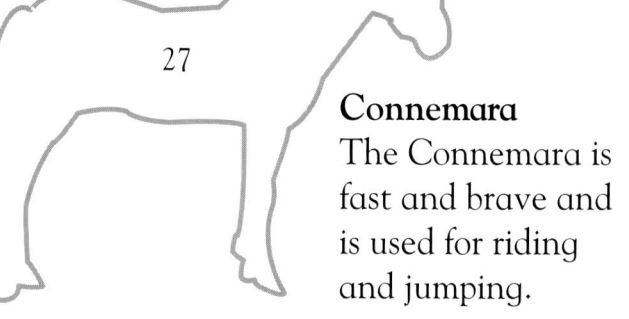

Connemara
The Connemara is fast and brave and is used for riding and jumping.

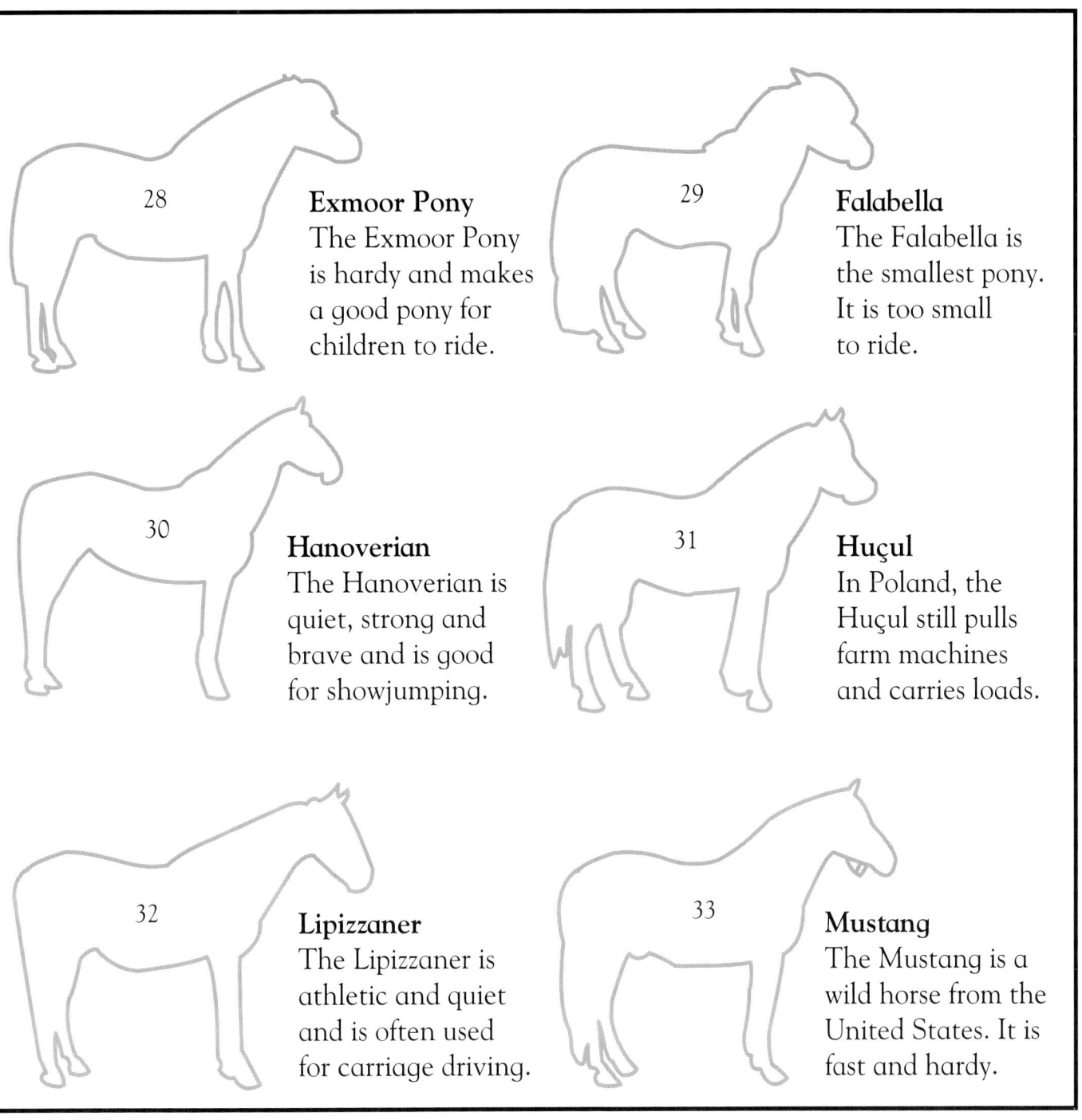

28 Exmoor Pony
The Exmoor Pony is hardy and makes a good pony for children to ride.

29 Falabella
The Falabella is the smallest pony. It is too small to ride.

30 Hanoverian
The Hanoverian is quiet, strong and brave and is good for showjumping.

31 Huçul
In Poland, the Huçul still pulls farm machines and carries loads.

32 Lipizzaner
The Lipizzaner is athletic and quiet and is often used for carriage driving.

33 Mustang
The Mustang is a wild horse from the United States. It is fast and hardy.

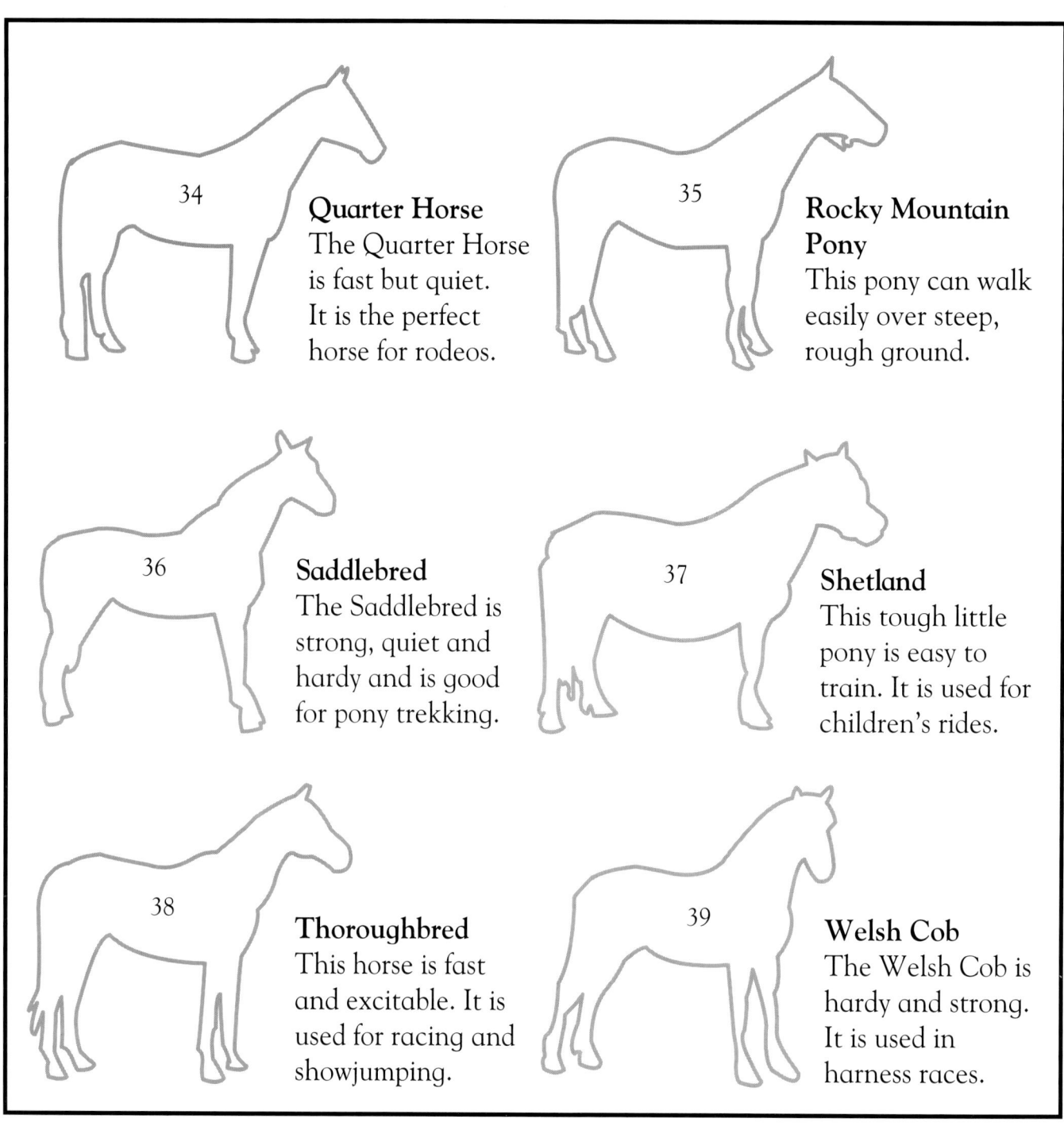

Quarter Horse
The Quarter Horse is fast but quiet. It is the perfect horse for rodeos.

Rocky Mountain Pony
This pony can walk easily over steep, rough ground.

Saddlebred
The Saddlebred is strong, quiet and hardy and is good for pony trekking.

Shetland
This tough little pony is easy to train. It is used for children's rides.

Thoroughbred
This horse is fast and excitable. It is used for racing and showjumping.

Welsh Cob
The Welsh Cob is hardy and strong. It is used in harness races.

FARM
ANIMALS

Pigs

Pigs grunt and snuffle in the sty. They use their strong snouts to root for food.

Fast asleep
Tiny piglets sleep in a heap together. The mother pig is careful not to roll on them.

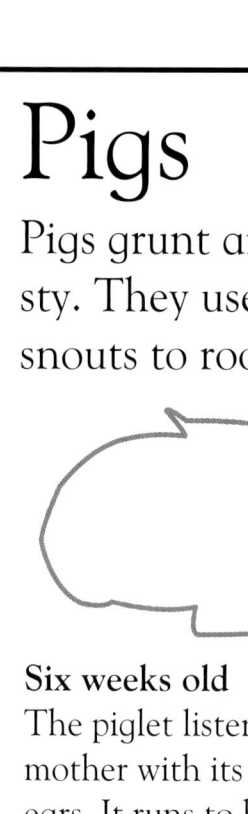

Tamworth pig
This hardy pig comes from the Midlands of England. It likes to live outdoors.

Six weeks old
The piglet listens for its mother with its large ears. It runs to her when she calls.

Two piglets
These two little piglets have just been born. One piglet is using the other as a comfortable pillow.

Making a nest
At night each pig burrows into the straw to make a comfy nest.

Mother's milk
The mother feeds her piglets with her milk. She lies down, and each piglet grabs a teat.

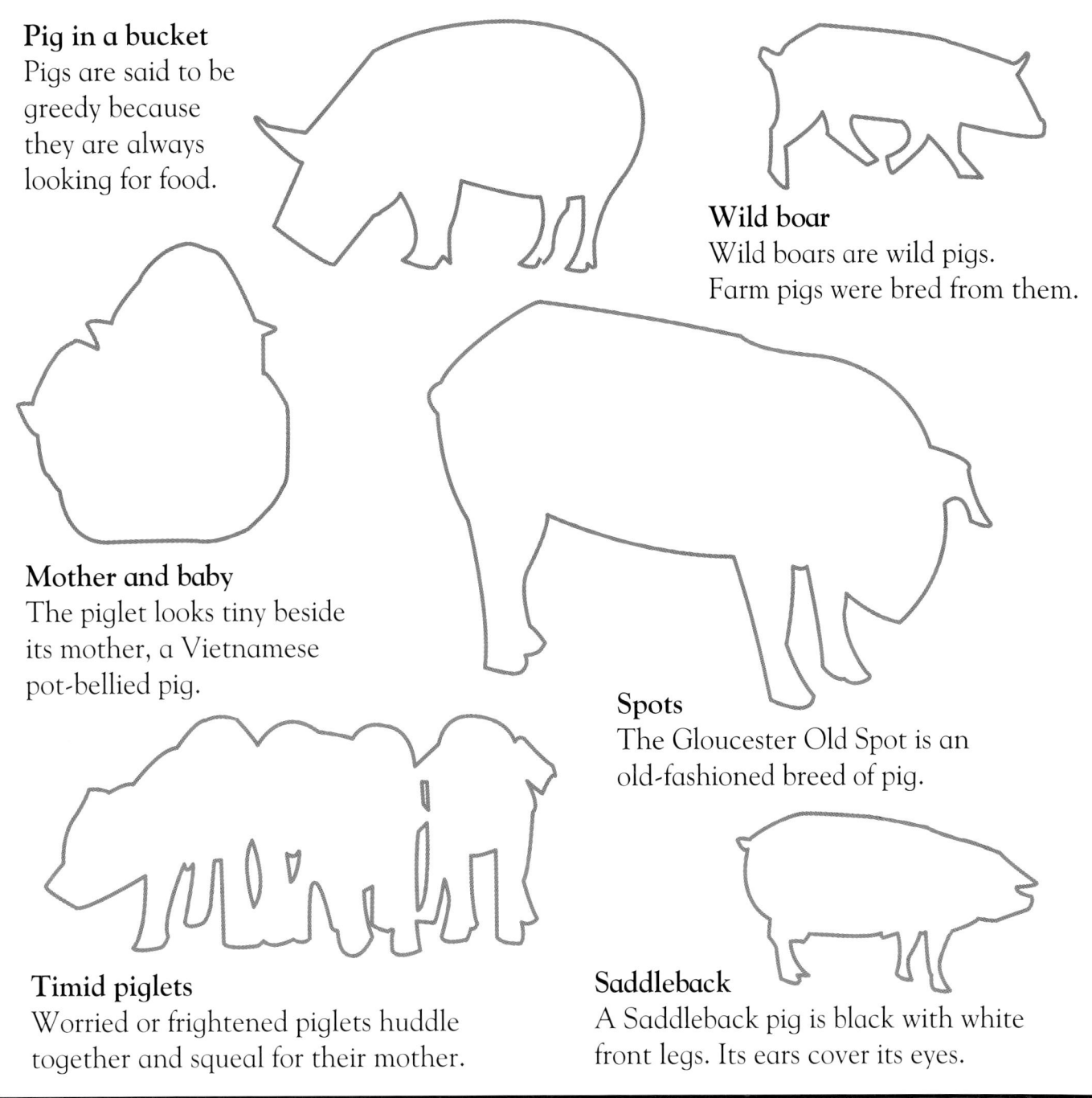

Pig in a bucket
Pigs are said to be greedy because they are always looking for food.

Wild boar
Wild boars are wild pigs. Farm pigs were bred from them.

Mother and baby
The piglet looks tiny beside its mother, a Vietnamese pot-bellied pig.

Spots
The Gloucester Old Spot is an old-fashioned breed of pig.

Timid piglets
Worried or frightened piglets huddle together and squeal for their mother.

Saddleback
A Saddleback pig is black with white front legs. Its ears cover its eyes.

Cows

Cows eat grass and hay. Later, they bring up cuds of food to chew again.

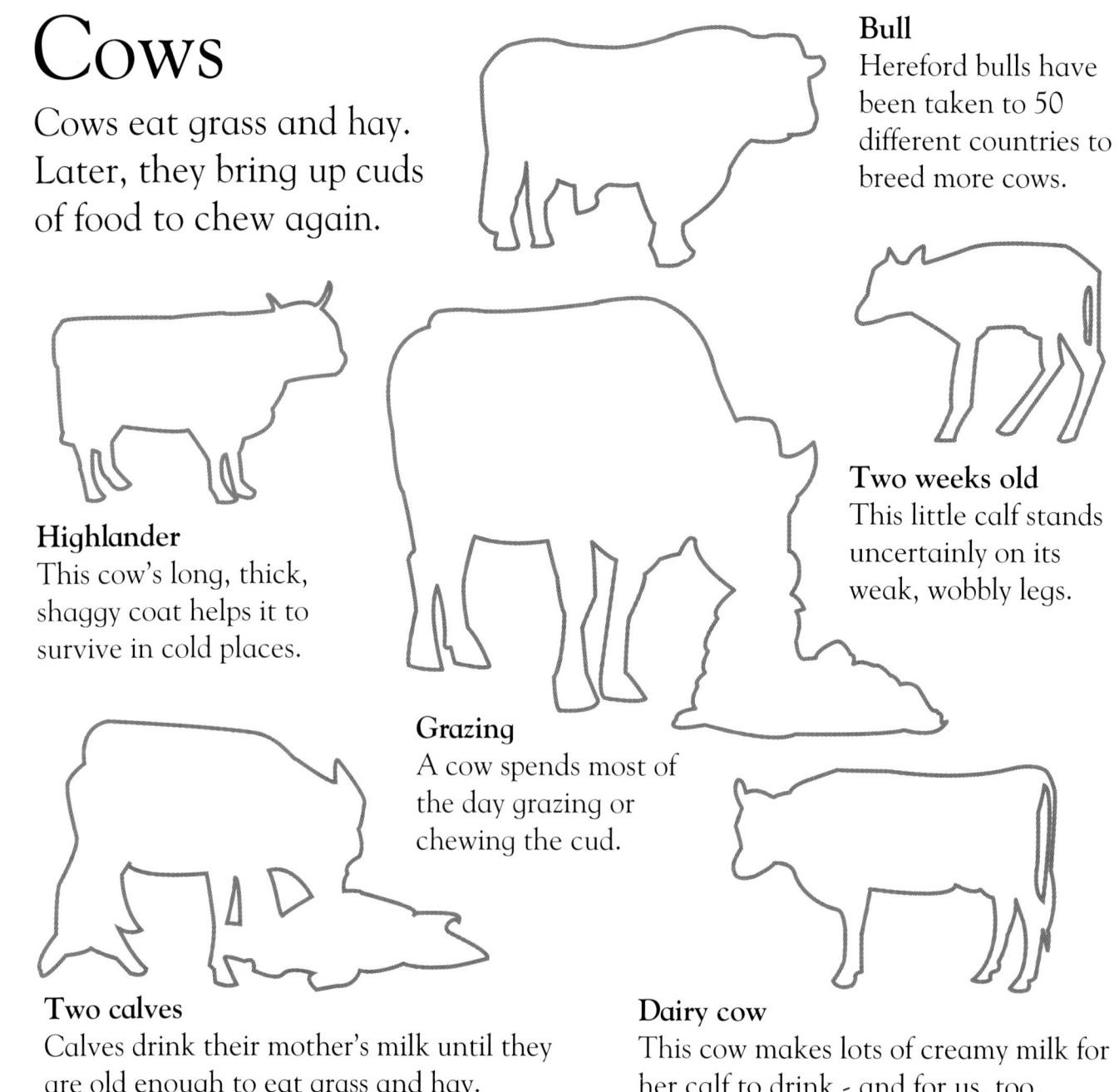

Bull
Hereford bulls have been taken to 50 different countries to breed more cows.

Highlander
This cow's long, thick, shaggy coat helps it to survive in cold places.

Two weeks old
This little calf stands uncertainly on its weak, wobbly legs.

Grazing
A cow spends most of the day grazing or chewing the cud.

Two calves
Calves drink their mother's milk until they are old enough to eat grass and hay.

Dairy cow
This cow makes lots of creamy milk for her calf to drink - and for us, too.

There are extra stickers on these pages just for fun.

There are extra stickers on these pages just for fun.

Sheep

Sheep have thick, woolly coats. They live in flocks on grassy fields and hills.

Curly coat
When the two lambs grow up they will have a shaggy, curly coat, just like their mother's.

Warm wool
A warm coat helps this sheep survive in the cold.

Black lamb
This black-faced sheep has an almost-black lamb. The male and female sheep both have horns.

Frolicking lambs
The lamb on the bale of hay likes to be king of the castle.

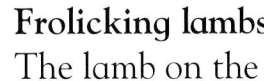

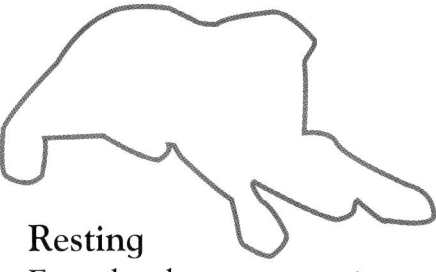

One week old
This little lamb is bleating for its mother.

Resting
Even lambs rest sometimes.

Time to eat
A lamb drinks milk from its mother's udder. The milk makes it grow big and strong.

Ducks and geese

No farmyard is complete without quacking ducks and cackling geese. They roam on the grass or swim in the pond.

German Saxony duck
This brown-and-white duck comes from the Saxony region of Germany.

Mother and babies
The mother duck is guarding her ducklings.

Honking goose
Geese are useful as watchdogs. They honk loudly when they see strangers.

Large geese
Geese are usually larger than ducks. Wild geese fly north in the spring to breed.

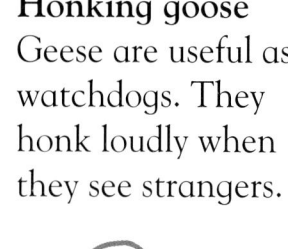

Runner ducks
Most ducks waddle, but these runner ducks scamper along.

Duckling
This fluffy duckling is only two days old.

Gosling
Goslings and ducklings both have webbed feet.

Chickens

A hen takes good care of her chicks both before and after they hatch from her eggs.

Just hatched
These tiny chicks have just pecked their way out of their shell. They look like little bundles of fluff!

Eight weeks old
This young chicken has lost its fluffy feathers.

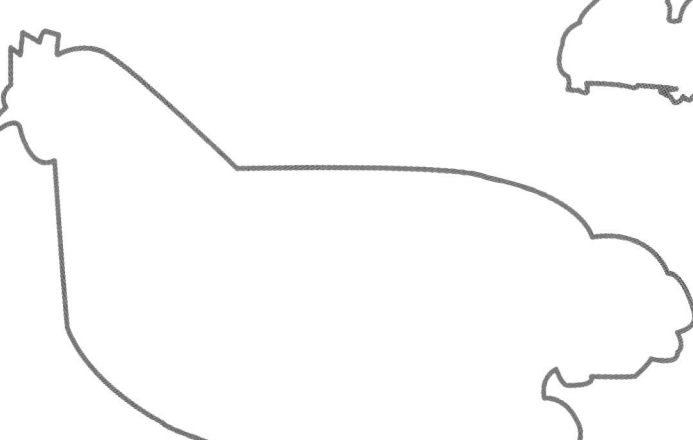

Laying an egg
A hen lays one or more eggs every day in a nesting box.

Fine feathers
A Buff Orpington chicken has lots of fine, long tail feathers.

Mother and brood
Chicks stay near their mother. They like to hide under her wings.

Eating seeds
Soon after they are born, chicks begin to eat seeds, just as their mother does.

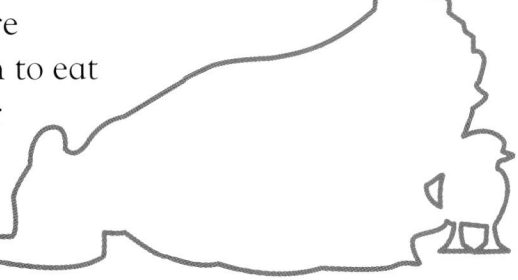

Horses

Horses used to pull carts and farm machinery. Today most horses are kept for riding.

Riding
The horse and rider enjoy an outing together.

Cart-horse
Cart-horses are bigger and stronger than most other horses.

Mother and foal
The newborn foal has just struggled to stand on its long, wobbly legs.

Apple thief!
Horses love sweet, crunchy apples. This little foal is helping itself from the bag.

Large foal
This foal is six months old and nearly as tall as its mother.

Two foals
These two foals have lost their mother, so one of them is whinnying for her.

CATS AND KITTENS

Kittens

Kittens love to play. They are learning the skills they will use as cats.

Balancing on a branch
Kittens and cats use their claws to cling to the wood and their tails to help them balance.

Outstretched paws
This black kitten has pounced on a fluffy toy chick. You can see it between its white paws.

Growing bigger
These cute little kittens have big eyes and fluffy fur. They will grow bigger and bigger.

Tabby twins
One of these kittens is bigger than the other.

Five little kittens
Most cats have four kittens in a litter, but some breeds have larger litters.

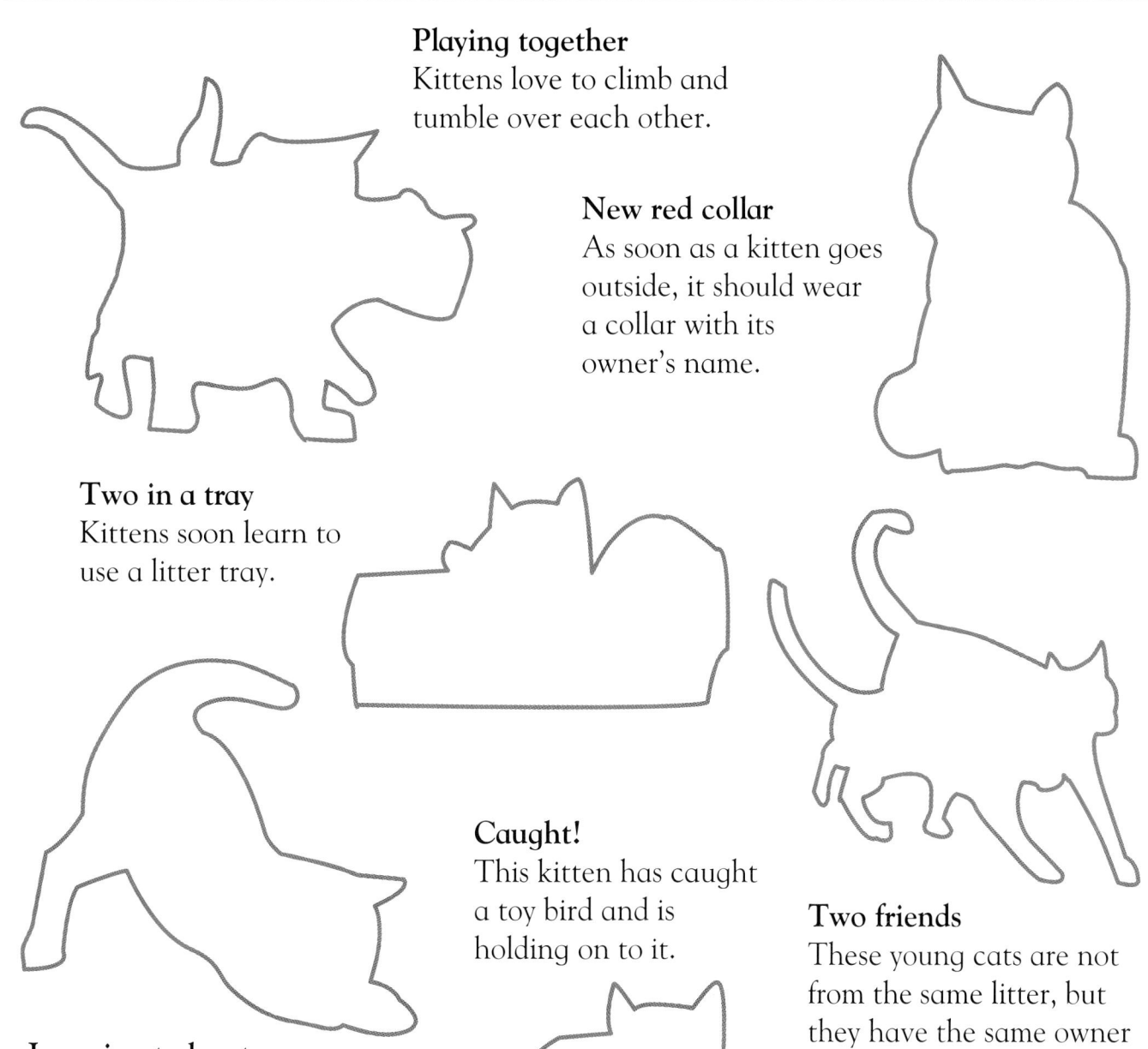

Playing together
Kittens love to climb and
tumble over each other.

New red collar
As soon as a kitten goes
outside, it should wear
a collar with its
owner's name.

Two in a tray
Kittens soon learn to
use a litter tray.

Caught!
This kitten has caught
a toy bird and is
holding on to it.

Two friends
These young cats are not
from the same litter, but
they have the same owner
and are good friends.

Learning to hunt
This eager kitten pounces
on anything that moves.

Long-haired cats

Long-haired cats need to be groomed every day to keep their fur tidy.

Brown Classic Tabbies
This British breed was one of the first to have a special cat club.

Pointed Longhair
A cat with dark tips and patches of fur is called *pointed*.

Norwegian Forest Cat
This cat's extra-thick, waterproof coat keeps it dry.

Angora
This breed originally came from Turkey.

Maine Coon
This is one of the largest cats. It originally came from Maine in New England.

Persian
This is one of the most popular long-haired cats.

There are extra stickers on these pages just for fun.

There are extra stickers on these pages just for fun.

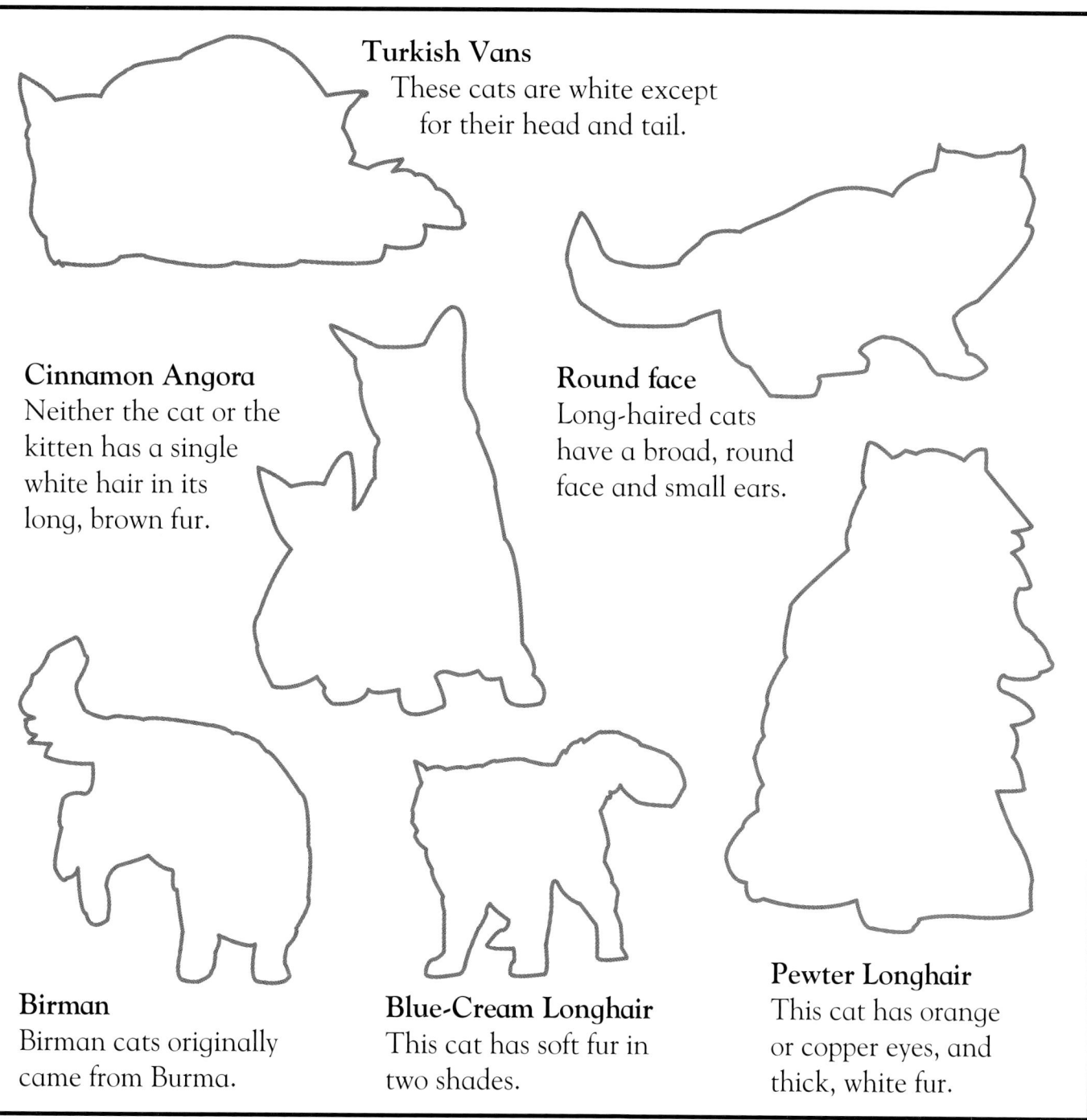

Turkish Vans
These cats are white except
for their head and tail.

Cinnamon Angora
Neither the cat or the
kitten has a single
white hair in its
long, brown fur.

Round face
Long-haired cats
have a broad, round
face and small ears.

Birman
Birman cats originally
came from Burma.

Blue-Cream Longhair
This cat has soft fur in
two shades.

Pewter Longhair
This cat has orange
or copper eyes, and
thick, white fur.

Short-haired cats

Most ordinary, domestic cats have short hair, not long hair. Pedigree short-haired cats are specially bred.

British Blue
Cat experts call this cat's smoky fur *blue*.

Short-haired friends
These two friends are non-pedigree cats.

Mother and kittens
These short-haired cats have a small head and long ears. The mother cat guards her kittens.

Abyssinian
This type of golden-brown cat was one of the first to be kept by people.

Tortoiseshell
Most tortoiseshell cats are female.

Russian Blue
This cat has a long tail and large ears. Its fur feels like seal's fur.

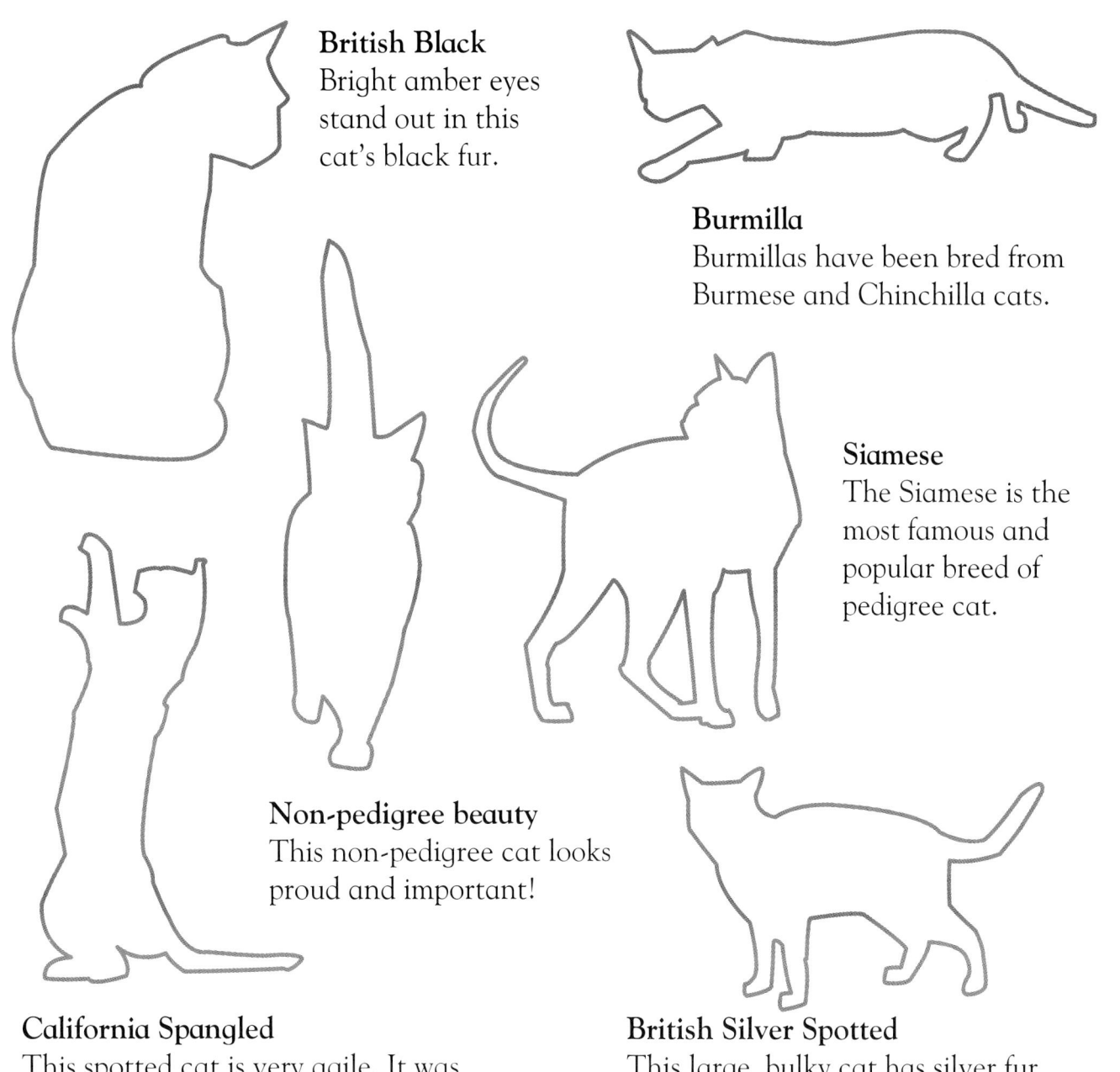

British Black
Bright amber eyes
stand out in this
cat's black fur.

Burmilla
Burmillas have been bred from
Burmese and Chinchilla cats.

Siamese
The Siamese is the
most famous and
popular breed of
pedigree cat.

Non-pedigree beauty
This non-pedigree cat looks
proud and important!

California Spangled
This spotted cat is very agile. It was
bred from many kinds of cat.

British Silver Spotted
This large, bulky cat has silver fur
with many black spots.

Playing

Cats love to play. This helps them get good at the skills they will need for hunting.

Hide and seek
Cats love to climb into an empty box.

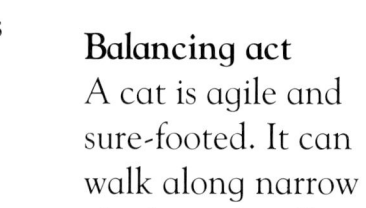

Saying hello
Cats greet each other by sniffing noses.

Sharp claws
A cat uses its claws and teeth to hold its prey.

Balancing act
A cat is agile and sure-footed. It can walk along narrow planks and walls.

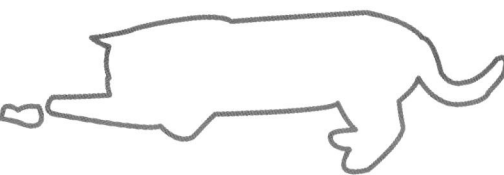

Scratching post
These cats have toys on their special post.

Leaping
A cat stretches to full length as it leaps.

Pouncing
One paw pushes the toy to see if it will move like live prey.

DOGS AND PUPPIES

Puppies

Puppies are cute, clumsy and adorable. They love to play and explore.

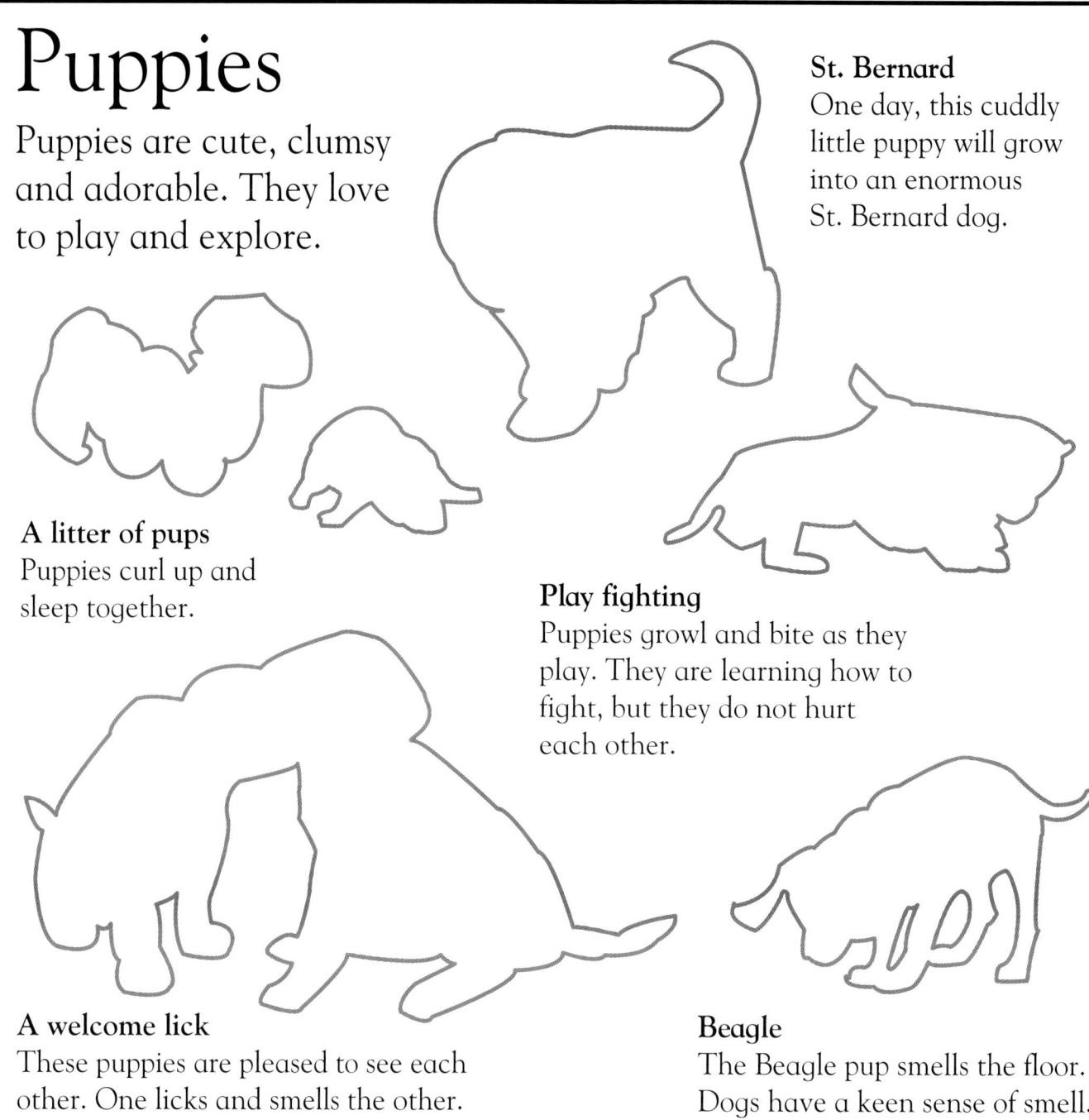

St. Bernard
One day, this cuddly little puppy will grow into an enormous St. Bernard dog.

A litter of pups
Puppies curl up and sleep together.

Play fighting
Puppies growl and bite as they play. They are learning how to fight, but they do not hurt each other.

A welcome lick
These puppies are pleased to see each other. One licks and smells the other.

Beagle
The Beagle pup smells the floor. Dogs have a keen sense of smell.

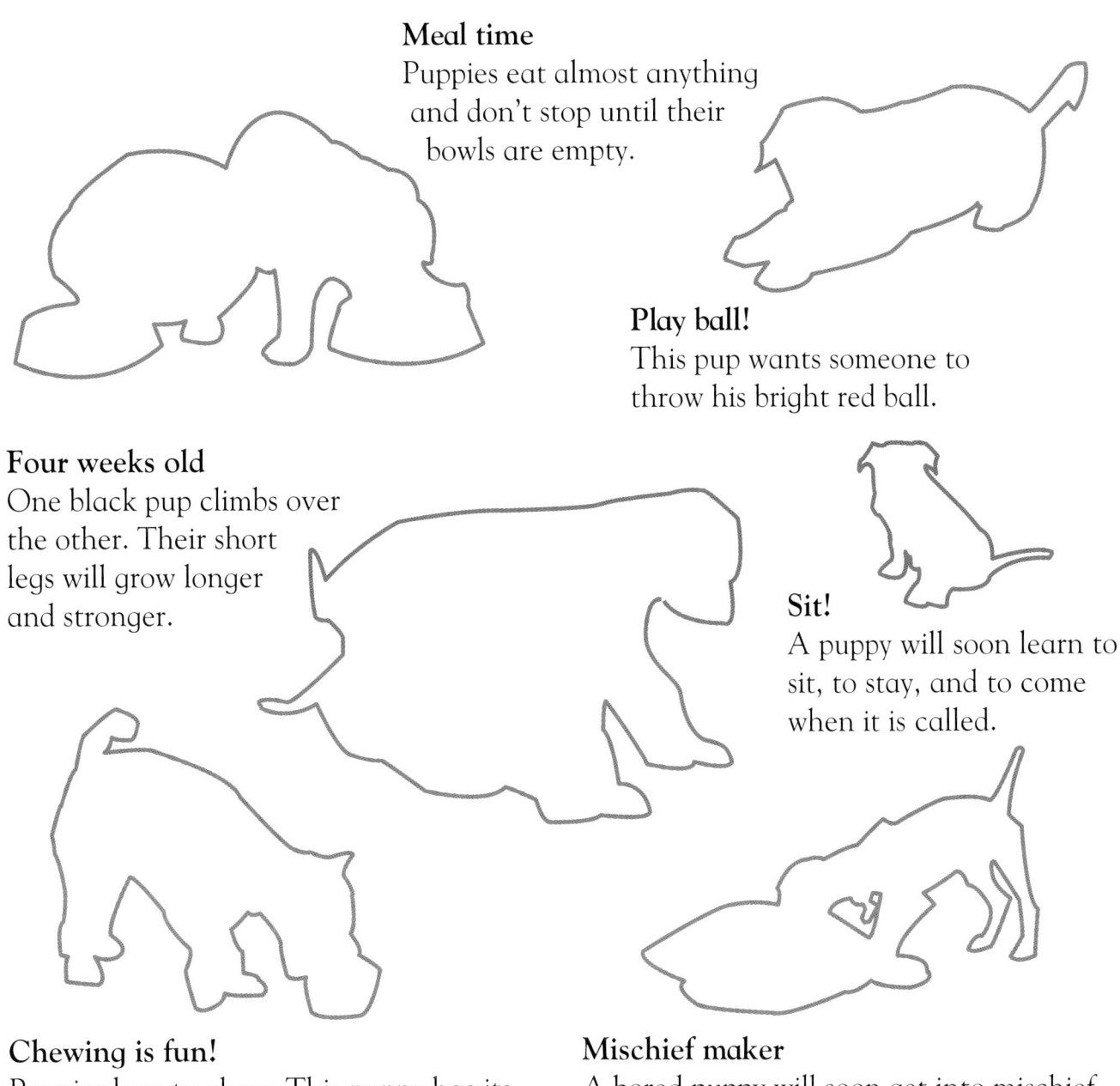

Meal time
Puppies eat almost anything
and don't stop until their
bowls are empty.

Play ball!
This pup wants someone to
throw his bright red ball.

Four weeks old
One black pup climbs over
the other. Their short
legs will grow longer
and stronger.

Sit!
A puppy will soon learn to
sit, to stay, and to come
when it is called.

Chewing is fun!
Puppies love to chew. This puppy has its
own toy to chew as much as it likes.

Mischief maker
A bored puppy will soon get into mischief.
This pup is making lots of mess!

Large dogs

Some large dogs are fierce guard dogs. Others are friendly, gentle giants.

Great Dane
A Great Dane looks even bigger when it stands up! It is very lively and loves children.

Segugio Italiano
This sleek dog with long, floppy ears was bred as a hunting dog.

Alaskan Malamute
This powerful dog was bred by the Inuit people to pull heavy loads.

Neopolitan Mastiff
A Mastiff is strong and extremely heavy.

Mastiff Wolf Hound
Large dogs are full of energy. They need lots of space and a long walk every day.

Dalmatians
Dalmatian puppies are born pure white and only develop their black spots later.

There are extra stickers on these pages just for fun.

There are extra stickers on these pages just for fun.

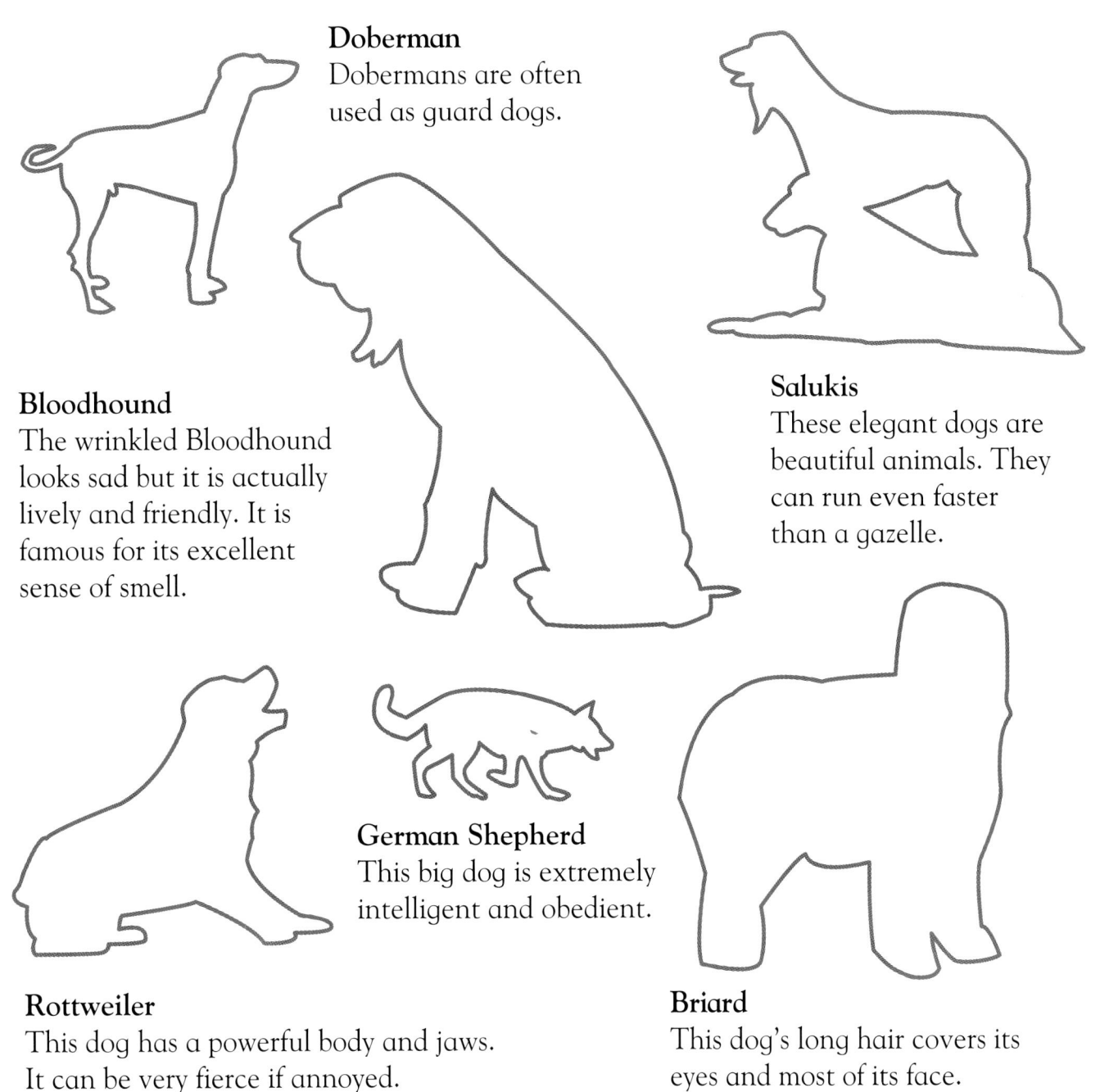

Doberman
Dobermans are often
used as guard dogs.

Bloodhound
The wrinkled Bloodhound
looks sad but it is actually
lively and friendly. It is
famous for its excellent
sense of smell.

Salukis
These elegant dogs are
beautiful animals. They
can run even faster
than a gazelle.

German Shepherd
This big dog is extremely
intelligent and obedient.

Rottweiler
This dog has a powerful body and jaws.
It can be very fierce if annoyed.

Briard
This dog's long hair covers its
eyes and most of its face.

Medium-sized dogs

These dogs usually make excellent pets. There are many different breeds.

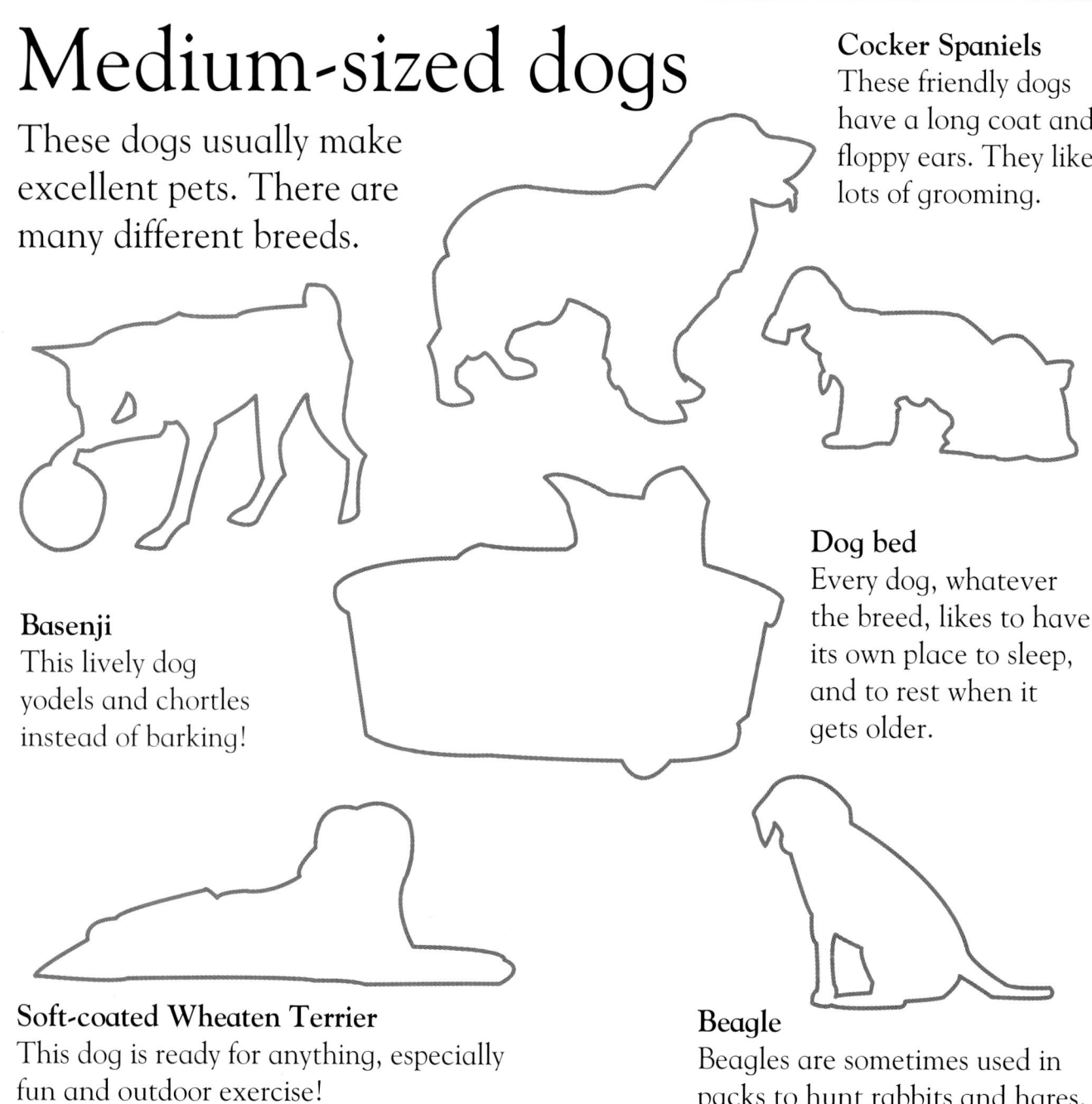

Cocker Spaniels
These friendly dogs have a long coat and floppy ears. They like lots of grooming.

Basenji
This lively dog yodels and chortles instead of barking!

Dog bed
Every dog, whatever the breed, likes to have its own place to sleep, and to rest when it gets older.

Soft-coated Wheaten Terrier
This dog is ready for anything, especially fun and outdoor exercise!

Beagle
Beagles are sometimes used in packs to hunt rabbits and hares.

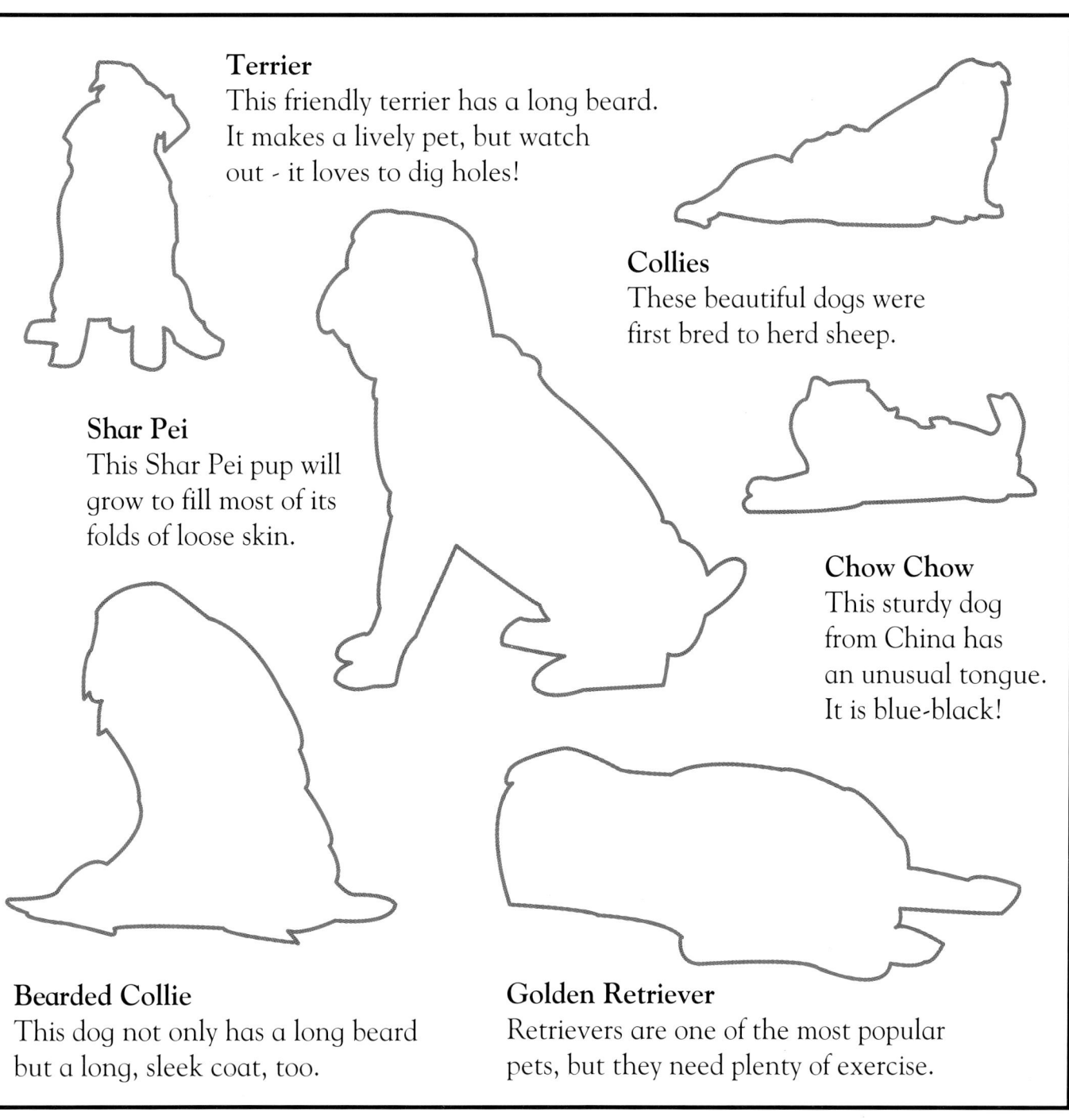

Terrier
This friendly terrier has a long beard.
It makes a lively pet, but watch
out - it loves to dig holes!

Collies
These beautiful dogs were
first bred to herd sheep.

Shar Pei
This Shar Pei pup will
grow to fill most of its
folds of loose skin.

Chow Chow
This sturdy dog
from China has
an unusual tongue.
It is blue-black!

Bearded Collie
This dog not only has a long beard
but a long, sleek coat, too.

Golden Retriever
Retrievers are one of the most popular
pets, but they need plenty of exercise.

Small dogs

Little dogs make loyal companions. Although small, they are lively.

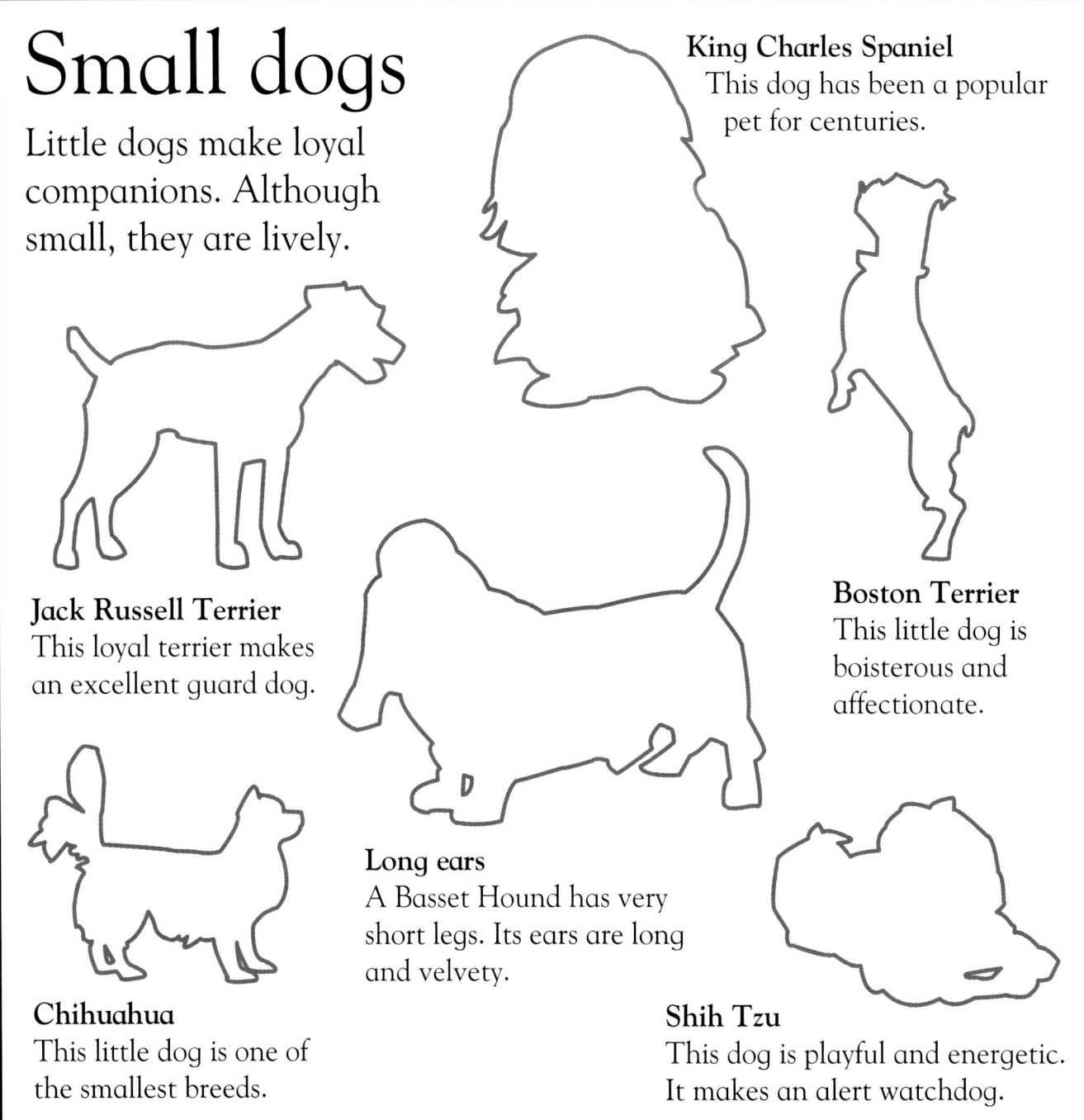

King Charles Spaniel
This dog has been a popular pet for centuries.

Jack Russell Terrier
This loyal terrier makes an excellent guard dog.

Boston Terrier
This little dog is boisterous and affectionate.

Long ears
A Basset Hound has very short legs. Its ears are long and velvety.

Chihuahua
This little dog is one of the smallest breeds.

Shih Tzu
This dog is playful and energetic. It makes an alert watchdog.